i

Travels in a Teacup

Paul Gunton

authorHOUSE®

AuthorHouse™ UK Ltd.
500 Avebury Boulevard
Central Milton Keynes, MK9 2BE
www.authorhouse.co.uk
Phone: 08001974150

First published by AuthorHouse 8/24/2009

ISBN: 978-1-4343-6375-6 (sc)
ISBN: 978-1-4343-6376-3 (hc)

Printed in the United States of America
Bloomington, Indiana

This book is printed on acid-free paper.

ACKNOWLEDGEMENTS

I wish to acknowledge with grateful thanks, the following organisations who kindly gave me permission to reproduce certain articles:-

Africa Tea Brokers, Mombasa, Kenya
Central Africana Limited, Blantyre, Malawi
Coastweek, Mombasa, Kenya
D.H.L. Express
Imperial War Museum, letter written by Mr M.G. Hibberd, Department of Exhibits and Firearms
Independent Organic Inspectorate
Kings World Trust for Children
Chaplain, Royal Air Force
Telegraph Media Group
Yachting Monthly

I would also like to thank Enid McBurney my patient secretary who gave me much encouragement and advice, Lorely Forrester, who gave valuable comments on the script and presentation and Naomi McBride who created the cover.

This book is for dear Cicely

Little did she know what she was in for on our Wedding Day but she has shared so many adventures in life and has created beautiful homes in every country where we have lived. I could not have wished for a more loving soul mate .....
Bless her.

CONTENTS

PREFACE

During two recent journeys, a Nun whose company I enjoyed as we travelled from Dublin to Ballymote and the Cabin Director on a Qatar Airlines flight, both repeated the comment made by relations and friends over the past few years that I should share my experiences in life by writing, for the enjoyment of others.

This is my first attempt at narrative writing, my previous experience simply being a monthly Tea Review for the Standard Chartered Bank and weekly Tea Market Letters that were sent worldwide and attracted far more interest from their topical, concluding paragraph than the content of the letters themselves, but my enjoyment in writing has spurred me to take pen to paper.

It has also given me time for thankful reflection on a life that has been unique in many respects and that, certainly, will not be experienced by anyone in the future given the multitude of changes worldwide during the past half century.

ENTER THE REAL WORLD

I received some sound advice from a family friend, a solicitor in New Bond Street, London as I set out to attend my interview at Harrisons and Crosfield Ltd in the City, "just picture the director in his bath", were the farewell words.

Two hours later, I was trying to do just that, but the surroundings were far removed from any bathroom and the Orcadian opposite was a stern character but with a kindly face that lit up as he viewed the photograph attached to my application form. My mother had given to me one of her photographs, taken with me at the helm of the family fishing boat, heading up the Helford River with a fine wake and Nare Point astern. Probably, the interview was not conducted on conventional lines, indeed it had a distinct nautical flavour but after some time, it was concluded with the more solemn words, "Well, Divinity 'O' level is not going to benefit you much in the Company but welcome on Monday when you will join finance and accounts department as an overseas trainee."

On 11th November, 1957 I began my first day as a paid employee and found my desk to be amongst a group of middle aged ladies who, during the next seven months, rarely smiled and carried the burden of commerce on their shoulders. Everyone signed the attendance book on arrival and it was removed exactly at 0925hrs so the arrival of any late employee was carefully noted, and during those months, no one was called by their first name. However, the time passed in interesting ways – I was mainly involved marrying indents and invoices, detailing thousands of orders for goods being shipped worldwide – Formica and Crittal metal windows were particularly large, continuing shipments to Borneo from the manufacturers in England. These orders had emanated from the Company offices in Brunei, North Borneo and Sarawak.

The day came when I moved to export department and said farewell to the sheltered ladies whose life was shattered shortly afterwards by my successor, who, in an idle moment, was tipping his chair backwards. Alas the two legs skidded on the shining linoleum, the chair shot forwards and he backwards, to crack his head on the desk behind, where he uttered one word … the F word. By the time that he extricated himself from the well of his own desk, removed the offending chair from his person and emerged triumphant, the ladies were gone, taking refuge in the corridor outside. Export department was more interesting but very short lived, less than a month, in fact, and then I moved to inward shipping department.

Here, I was involved mainly with tea documentation for tea manufactured by the Company managed estates in India, Indonesia and Ceylon, destined for the London weekly tea auctions conducted in Mincing Lane. Teas shipped from Calcutta, Cochin and Colombo were handled, on arrival, by several tea warehouses throughout the London docks and whose individual warehouse warrants were documents, the likes of which I have never seen anywhere else – their individual designs, colourings and wording were unique and would be collector's items today.

Almost on my first anniversary of joining the Company, I was asked if I would like to fill a vacancy in the Tea department, to follow a definite career, rather than a general trading position anywhere abroad. I made the immediate decision to accept and launched in to the Tea Trade for a career that was to span forty five years, as a tea taster, buyer, blender, broker and consultant.

The Tea department was directed by a Board member of the Company, a bachelor who had spent years in Calcutta and who had obviously spent a colourful life. Some years after his retirement an old group photograph was unearthed with his motto under a beaming face reading, (in Hindi) "May your member ever be strong." This rather portly gentleman arrived in the department one morning, dressed in a three piece suit and wearing his traditional bow tie, to be drawn up short at the sight of my fellow trainee (ex Guards) wearing a rose in his button hole. "Take – that – flower – off – your – person" boomed the words through the department. "But, but, sir" came the stuttered reply, "Today is St. George's Day." "I do not mind what day of the year it is … the scent will impair the quality of the teas." The rose was removed smartly, the trainee later resigned before being offered a position abroad, but he retained his links with the Trade and became the manager of the Tea Hotel in Kericho, Kenya. The manager of the Tea department was a kindly person who had spent some war years as a P.O.W. in Indonesia and the department supervisor was a Scotsman who sported a very long drooping moustache, a real walrus example.

There were four London based staff and one other overseas trainee but the days were filled with interest and tasting started from the very first. Tea samples were received daily by airmail from all the major tea producing countries, some from the company tea departments in Calcutta, Cochin, Colombo and Djkarta, representing teas manufactured by the company administered tea estates, offers from the company trading offices in those centres, including Taipei, and offer samples from many other trading offices worldwide and in the United Kingdom. All these samples had to be sorted, tasted and evaluated, with many offer samples being posted to potential buyers and tea blenders by the close of business each day. Also there were many samples delivered by the London tea warehouse companies representing company teas shipped from origin, unsold, to be catalogued for sale in the Mincing Lane tea auction centre and these samples, too, had to be tasted, evaluated and discussed with the nominated tea broker entrusted with the sale of every invoice.

However, my days in Head office were numbered and in June 1959, I was appointed assistant manager to the Company tea department in Cochin, South India. On my last working day in London, I said a fond farewell to all those people with whom I had worked, including the mail room staff who were assisted on a rota basis by the overseas trainees, handling all the daily sacks of incoming mail from around the world: the postage stamps in those days were colourful and beautifully designed and there was much competition for them amongst several budding stamp collectors.

SOUTH OF GOA

I, the merchant adventurer, stepped on to Indian soil on the 7th July 1959 aged twenty and within two years of leaving school, and having signed a four year contract with no provision for leave outside India, I was not destined to see home until 1963.

The journey from London had been straight forward but over twenty four hours on an Air India Super Constellation, and my time in the Taj Mahal Hotel in Bombay was brief, as the Indian Airlines flight, by D.C.3 left shortly after 0600 hrs bound for Cochin. The aircraft challenged the South West Monsoon throughout the journey, conditions at times, were very rough but we arrived safely in the lashing rain where I was met by my manager, a great character who had been in the Tea trade many years. Luncheon followed at the general manager's bungalow before I was driven to the Harrisons and Crosfield chummery set at the mouth of the harbour, so every ship entering or leaving port, literally, sailed past the property and the famed Chinese fishing nets lining the foreshore.

A chummery, by tradition, is a bachelor pad and I was to share with two other expatriates, one employed in the shipping department, the other in the (Tea and Rubber) Estates department. We each had our own bedroom and bathroom, but shared the dining room and upstairs sitting room with a commanding view of the harbour entrance. The company provided hard furnishings and this term was literal, for when a wooden tub bath was replaced one year, no conventional unit could be found, so management had built a concrete replacement – bloody for the skin if you slid in too eagerly. A ton and a half of cut wood per month served the wood stove which was the sole cooking facility and also provided for hot water, the water being heated in a large cauldron in a building at the back of the garden and then carried in buckets to the baths when required, whilst the refrigerator operated on paraffin.

To administer the establishment, a staff of seven was employed. The head bearer, Annie, was elderly but so loyal and would never retire to bed until the last of us had arrived home, catnapping in an armchair beside the front door before he locked up. He also guided me quietly during my first year. I used to tell him when I was dining out and requested certain clothes to be laid out on my bed but when the bath had been drawn, and I had been summoned, I would be met by Annie at the bedroom door with a slight bow and a discreet cough … "As master is dining out with Madam so-and-so tonight, (he already knew, Cochin being such a small expatriate community), does not master consider he should wear so-and-so instead?" I usually agreed, the clothes selected were already laid out, and I arrived more suitably groomed for the occasions.

The three of us were invited to a ship's party one night and whilst we were changing, there was a dramatic thunderstorm with a bolt of lightning and an immediate clap. My bath water sounded exactly like soda water when the bottle top is flipped and the whole area was plunged in to pitch darkness. All was not lost … Shortly afterwards Annie was padding down the corridor in the light of a candle with three stout whiskies on a tray – I hoped that he had enjoyed one too.

We also employed an assistant bearer, the cook, the dhobi, who washed and ironed immaculately, the water carrier, the Mali -gardener, and the sweeper. Electricity was our source of lighting and fans kept us cool – air conditioners were rare fixtures and for young bachelors, financially out of reach.

A mile along the water front were the Company offices, Tea department on the right hand side, on the first floor of a building with tea godowns (warehouses) below, whilst opposite, the rest of the Company's interests were established up to the wharf and the jetty where the 'African Queen' type launch was moored.

THE CHUMMERY
FORT COCHIN KERALA STATE

THE VIEW FROM THE SITTING ROOM WINDOW

CHINESE FISHING NETS

AN EVENING LANDFALL

The office operated five and a half days a week and with no transport provided, I immediately purchased a bicycle for sixty rupees. The journeys were always eventful, weaving in and out of the other bicycles, vehicles, goats, rickshaws, handcarts, people and more people and in the Monsoon, the fierce bursts of rain could often be avoided by a careful look to seaward, south westwards; however, it was often sobering to be passed by my manager (who lived literally next door), in the rain, as he was driven to work in the department car, a Standard 10. Such was the form, twelve years after the country had gained her independence.

Tea department commanded a position as one of the leading tea exporters from Cochin with respected accounts in Canada, east and west coasts, America, Chile, Australia, New Zealand, England, Ireland, Holland, Germany, and Malta in particular. All teas for buyers were purchased in the weekly, Tuesday, Cochin auctions and the auctioneers were alert. A labrador was brought into the auction room one morning by the wife of a buyer out for a walk and spying his master and excited by the bidding, he barked. "Is that a bid sir?" came the immediate response: Tempter, the labrador was walked home. Teas were shipped in their original tea chests packed by the tea estates, or floor blended. The tea chests from several estates were opened, up to one hundred chests per blend, as selected by the office tea tasters and blenders and detailed on the blending sheet, and the contents of all, spilled out to create a pyramid. Men with wooden spades turned the pyramid three times to create a uniform blend, before repacking the tea into the same chests, after which these chests were scraped of their original markings and stencilled as per buyer's instructions. Pallets and containers had yet to be introduced so chests were moved individually and loaded aboard ships in rope slings.

Shipping opportunities were frequent to most destinations. An exceptional order was purchased one Tuesday morning, and as I cycled home that evening, I stopped to watch the New Zealand shipping company vessel Waitaki outward bound to Auckland with that order aboard and a very satisfied tea buyer at destination. Another exceptional, swift shipment followed the visit of an Arab gentleman to the department, who came, saw, bought and paid cash for fifty chests of tea, before berthing his own dhow alongside the company jetty and with customs formalities complete, literally set sail for home the next day.

In addition to exporting tea, the department was heavily involved with the tea produced by Malayalam Plantations numbering over twenty tea factories, tasting and evaluating their invoices throughout the year and recommending changes in manufacture where necessary. To drive home this message, a visiting Malayalam Plantations director from London said to me ... "Do not forget young laddie, an extra penny per pound, is a hundred thousand pounds per annum for the Company." Having delivered this message to the young laddie from tea department, he sidled away to more senior members of the community attending the Company cocktail party organized in his honour.

Department staff totalled ten and we were kept busy all the year round but from a tasting angle, one really had to spend a whole year at the counter before gaining continuity, basically due to the changing seasons and the tea produced every day. The second year round, though, basic knowledge had been gained of the individual estate's production and as time passed further, tea tasters could begin to recognize each estate by their leaf and liquor qualities. Tea production in South India is unique, embracing districts in three states, Karnataka, Tamil Nadu and Kerala with tea, (now replanted with rubber) then growing in a depression on Kundai Estate, Kerala, below sea level, to over 8,000 ft on the highest tea estate in the world, Kolukkumalai Estate, Tamil Nadu. Consequently the quality of tea varies considerably, each elevation and district reflecting distinct characteristics, and influenced, too, by the seasonal weather patterns.

Labour relations were cordial almost throughout the four years but the Company did have the dubious distinction of having the first labour strike, in 1961, but we did not close and with the addition of two other staff from the Head office in Quilon, nine of us did the work of one hundred and one people. However, having cycled part of the journey each day up to a warehouse handling lemon grass oil, I then had to dismount, face the less pleasant odours in the clinging humidity and take the plunge through the shouting throng, that sometimes shook full fountain pens at our backs. One morning, I was instructed to supervise a truck loading coffee for a shipment to Russia from the Company godown on Willingdon Island. 'Rent a Crowd' beat me to it but I managed to have the roll doors opened just sufficiently for the Mercedes truck to back through before jamming both doors tight against the cab. We completed loading, inside, to a ringing chorus outside of 'Resign and go back to school', so much for being the youngest expatriate on the staff.

Tea stock taking was always a trial – every tea chest had to be tallied in the heat of the metal roofed godowns and although office kit was long socks, shorts and short sleeved shirts, we needed to keep the fluid levels up and consumption of water and tea were always high. However, literally thousands of chests had to be counted by the staff and one afternoon an individual chest was unaccounted for, until the General Manager moved – he had been sitting on it – he bought us all a beer in the evening.

The Cochin club (members only) was the centre of the community, set in two acres of gardens, beside the foreshore with tennis courts and a squash court, whilst inside, the large bar was a constant, welcome, watering hole next to the billiard room offering two tables, with well stocked library and a ballroom / theatre beyond. It was a well managed establishment where many happy hours were spent and where business was rarely discussed. The expatriate community numbered up to sixty at any one time, including the wives, so whilst everyone's social life was fairly common knowledge, business matters were respected. Every member was obliged to apply for a liquor licence to comply with the law but there was only one member whose place at the bar was hallowed ground and as evenings grew long, he traditionally broke into the (same) song ... "Drake is sailing westwards lads, the ships are in the bay" ...

My first evening in Fort Cochin coincided with the weekly club evening on Wednesdays, all gentlemen were required to wear long ties, and I was able to meet the people with whom I was to live for the next four years. There were no misfits, a reflection of the recruitment systems, and latterly, as I made my number with the most senior people, I found their company stimulating – some had served in India over thirty years. Their wives were treated with respect and reserve and after ten days – despite having met them all – I was obliged to write to them individually advising of my arrival in station and to deliver the letters in person, (on my bicycle), the letters being received by their head bearer. However, underneath all their dignity, they each had soft spots and Eve Northey, the wife of one of the most senior members of the community swept up four of us bachelors, taught us the basics of bridge and then launched us on to the bridge circle – not all at once though.

All parties had their memories but Christmas 1961 was probably one of the most enjoyable, when it was agreed that Father Christmas should arrive on an elephant as a surprise for everyone really. However, the elephant arrived two hours early but the Lipton manager kindly offered parking space in the bungalow garden. The mahout promptly went to sleep but the elephant was quite overcome with his luxurious surroundings, fixing his eye on a papaya tree and starting with the leaves he worked slowly downwards eating everything until the thickness of the lower trunk was not worth any further effort. However, all was not lost for he left a very generous deposit to enrich the garden and the triumphal procession set off for the club, preceded by the elderly town fire engine. Father Christmas, a leading shipping manager, became increasingly agitated atop the elephant as he began plodding up the drive, realizing that clearance under the portico would be very tight indeed but nothing was stopping the elephant, including the crowd gathered for the Christmas party. At ten yards there was no turning back, Father Christmas slid half way down the elephant's flank, clutching the sack of toys and as soon as they emerged through the portico, eager hands were ready to push Father Christmas back to his perch and restore his dignity.

A few days later the New Year's Party was held in the Ballroom, and one of my chummery companions lined up twelve pink gins along the bar and as each 'strike' of midnight was called, he 'downed' one glass, remained standing for some ten minutes and then retired to the bed of canna lilies, returning to the party before dawn. However, fierce drinking was rare and most entertaining was done in the home and Sunday curry lunch parties were always a hot favourite.

On one occasion, England was playing India in Bombay at the Brabourne Stadium and the visitors were not doing well so 'mine host' picked up the telephone and asked to be connected to the England captain. Remarkably, as even local calls were unobtainable or unreliable, Ted Dexter responded four hours later and 'mine host' was able to assure him that a loyal group of supporters was gathered in Cochin listening to every ball to wish the XI all possible success. Our support was warmly received with fraternal greetings. I, in fact, joined Lodge Cochin on the 21st October 1961, never to regret the day and as the Masonic Lodge is situated under the palm trees, beside the beach, the meetings were conducted to a background of surf breaking on the sand.

The Malabar sailing club (est 1896) that I represented at the Golden Jubilee Regatta of the Royal Madras Yacht Club in 1960 generated much pleasure, with evening racing on a Wednesday and afternoon racing on Saturdays, during the season, January – April, in the Company boat Curlew an 18 ft gaffed rigged, bamboo sparred, half decked, Naini Tal Class, one of eight in the club. There was also fine cruising on the back waters and the sailing programme could be drawn up in the knowledge that every day would be fine throughout the season, the sea breeze dying by noon and the land breeze starting by 1400 hrs. One year, I was offered an uncompleted dinghy by the crew of the British ship Clan Alpine that I imported and finished building from kit form. The Clan Alpine then sailed from Cochin to Chittagong where she was driven up river by a tidal bore to be beached high and dry a long distance from the water's edge, so my dinghy, later named Comorin was off loaded in the nick of time for otherwise she would have been abandoned.

I was taught to swim when I was nine years old and I have enjoyed swimming all my life but the only swimming pool in the vicinity was situated at the Malabar Hotel on Willingdon Island across the harbour,

THE COCHIN CLUB

COCHIN KERALA STATE
THE OFFICE COMPLEX ON WILLINGDON ISLAND
TEA DEPARTMENT NEAREST (SIX WINDOWS)

so unable to finance a car, I had built a canvas covered canoe to reach the pool, much to the misgivings of old hands who were heard to mutter that the likes of us were not seen in such craft. However, Petronella was the greatest success, she was copied seven times, two of which were built for Czechoslovakian crane erectors in the port who had previously been bored stiff, sitting for hours on the Malabar Hotel lawn. Water activities were limited though during the South West Monsoon, for not only were the days very wet but the volume of water in the harbour increased significantly. Odd nautical opportunities did present themselves, though, one being the Saturday morning I launched Petronella into the monsoon flood water opposite St. Francis Church, paddled down the road, through the Club gates, across the lawn to moor to a half submerged canna lily and a traditional lunch time beer followed. The Church is a historic building, known worldwide and where Vasco Da Gama was buried and I felt very humble to be invited to conduct the Sunday service once a month for a period, much to the pleasure of my uncle who was then Rural Dean of Sutton Coldfield. Whilst he was in office, his wife died, my aunt Mary, mother's youngest sister, and in Holy Trinity Church there is a stained glass window, dedicated to her memory.

We kept really very fit on the whole and there were three doctors in Cochin, two qualified and one not, but we preferred to use his expertise and after all his notepaper did give us some confidence, "MB BA (Failed)". On two occasions I did not call him to the Chummery, once when I had a fever and waking up in the small hours, having soaked the bed in perspiration, the door opened and in came the chokra, or junior house boy with a change of sheets and pillowcases – loyal Annie had instructed him to wait outside my door and as soon as he heard movement to come in and effect the change over. On another occasion I had the dreaded runs at night and I only made destination on the eighth occasion by crawling across the floor, all strength gone for walking. However the doctor was called to the chummery one morning and made a great performance of sterilising the thermometer and glass, at the base with cotton wool and diluted Dettol but the effect was short lived for

MALABAR SAILING CLUB
PRIZEGIVING DINNER 1962

VENUE: THE COCHIN CLUB BALLROOM

RECEIVING THE JOURDAIN JUG FROM THE COMMODORE'S WIFE
MRS ELSIE NICHOL

1961 WINNER: THE MAHARAJA OF TRAVANCORE CUP

1961 WINNER: THE COMMODORE'S CUP

1962 WINNER: THE JOURDAIN JUG

1976 WINNER: THE MALABAR SAILING CLUB CHALLENGE CUP

in one swift movement, he took the instrument from the glass, shook it, dried it under his sweaty armpit and popped it in to my open mouth. A visit to his surgery was an experience where swabs were tossed into the street. I cannot imagine what my mother would have thought, the fourth lady doctor to qualify from Durham University in 1922. Our dentist was young, German trained and resourceful for he extended the life of his limited instruments by removing the rust with sand paper and extracted one of my wisdom teeth in a brilliant operation … A local anaesthetic, no X-ray, right knee on my chest, pliers in, one fierce pull and out she came, hook, line and sinker.

However towards the end of 1962 I realized that I was becoming jaded, physically and mentally but not as bad as one of my Chummery companions who answering his desk telephone, spoke his name, then louder, and louder again only to realize that he had yet to pick up the receiver. True, our social life was enhanced by organised sporting weekends with the numerous tea estate expatriates and talented Indians and also, parties on merchants' ships, one that ended with a rickshaw race to the club from the jetty to where we had been ferried – much to the rickshaw drivers' delight. They were lined up across the road and at the signal, all competitors ran across, jumped in their nominated rickshaw and everyone set off – except one, who was a very well built man rather different from the driver who shot straight up in to the air, through the shafts. The machine flipped upside down, wheels spinning with the passenger beneath but order was restored and although last at the club, the driver was well compensated. We also had the delights of the Star Talkies to enjoy, the only cinema nearby situated in Mattancherri, once believed to be the most densely populated square mile in the World. As the footlights were switched on, the theatre dimmed and the stage curtains opened the resident rats raced off the stage but none, fortunately, ever jumped into the auditorium. Also, film reels were sometimes mixed up with cowboys meeting dramatic deaths then suddenly reappearing as large as life half an hour later – all added entertainment.

Furlough beckoned and I was in the air homeward bound in February 1963.

HOME SWEET HOME

My parents were at Heathrow to welcome me and it was good to see them looking so happy and fit. I did wonder about them constantly during the four years particularly as mother was thirty nine years old and father fifty when I was born, but I need not have worried. Probably of more importance, was what to expect of me when I came through the custom's hall after almost four years in the tropics.

We made our way home to Cornwall and the first week I kept bumping into the walls and pictures, promptly straightened by father, for two Chummery rooms would almost have accommodated their cottage. We discussed plans for my six months furlough and after two months, I set off on my first visit to Ireland, prompted by a family from Cochin who was also on furlough in Galway and a great friend of my parents who had bought our family home near the Lizard and whose daughter and family lived in Sligo.

On the midnight mailboat from Liverpool to Dublin I struck up conversation with folk beside me, ex tea planters from Kerala in the Company managed by my employers. The night passed quickly and another invitation was extended to stay with them in Connemara, so once my Sunbeam Rapier had been unslung from the ship, I made a decision to set off for Sligo, and then drive South to the other two families.

I noted that the journey took me through Longford, the home town of a Nun in Cochin who monthly, came to the office to collect tea that we donated to her convent. She had left home eighteen years before and had not seen her folk since, so begged me to make contact with them if I did visit her town. I pulled up in the main street, opened the window in the pouring rain and enquired where the family lived. A mischievous fella grinned and replied "Are you after the wife, sir, she's a fine woman?" – the nun's sister. Anyway I was directed to the right place – a prosperous general shop above which resided the family. My reception was very moving … Telephone calls were made and nearly thirty relatives gathered to meet the first living contact in eighteen years with their far flung relative, from Granny to a baby in arms. I bade my farewell after three hours leaving a very contented group and of course a few weeks later, I was back in Cochin, with first hand news of her family, joyously received too.

What my parents' friend in Cornwall had not told me, was that his daughter and family had returned as tea planters from Kerala in 1953 to take over the family farm – information that was exchanged within ten minutes of my arrival to our mutual amazement. However what no one could have foretold was that night I met their eldest daughter Cicely, who 'for better or worse' became my wife and in 2007 we celebrated our Ruby Wedding. I have often thought back to that day in 1963 – was it the Nun who played a part in our destiny?

I travelled back to Cornwall, via Galway and Connemara and spent the rest of my furlough around the Helford River. Alas, the artist 'Powder' Thorburn had passed on in his nineties but I have never forgotten his kindness four years earlier at his Frenchman's Creek studio when he gave me one of his oil paintings of the River entitled 'Secondary Approaching' with the comment that I would not forget my childhood play ground. Parents were in the process of moving house, Cicely came to spend a week in Cornwall and then I was Cochin bound – the furlough had been a happy period and I was mentally and physically rejuvenated.

A CHANGING YEAR

It was good to be back in station and pick up the business and social strings again – not much had changed but there was a wind of change in the air with more expatriates leaving for good, a situation that accelerated when the Indian rupee was devalued. Meantime, the Company had a major step ahead, moving from their long established premises on the mainland, to a newly built complex on Willingdon Island. This move was accomplished remarkably smoothly but it did mean that the Company launch took us across the harbour and back every day – no more cycling a weaving course along the waterfront to the office. Also, no more luncheons at the chummery, so I took a daily picnic lunch to the office, swam at the Malabar Hotel pool midday, and three days a week, conducted swimming lessons for the children attending the Cochin Club school.

The wind of change soon blew my way for in May 1964, I was appointed Manager, Tea and Coffee Department, Auckland, New Zealand. I had arrived in Cochin with my sole possessions packed in two suitcases and really did not have a great deal more when I packed two tin trunks and a Kashmiri chest.

I spent six weeks in England to see Cicely and parents who had settled into a delightful cottage between Penzance and Lands End, in sound of the sea through the wooded valley to the foreshore at St Lois. The Company arranged for me to spend time with a leading City coffee trading house for whom the Company acted as Broker in New Zealand – this Company continues to send me their regular coffee reports. My journey to Auckland was routed through Colombo, to familiarise myself, briefly, with that tea market and the next permanent touch down was Wellington where the company head office was situated.

AOTEAROA - THE LAND OF
THE LONG WHITE CLOUD

I t had been agreed that I would stay my first ten days in the Auckland Club, only a short walk from the office in Fort Street that was staffed by a very welcoming number of people. A company car was provided and my salary just over four figures per annum – any salary up to NZ£1000.00 obliged the employee to join a union apparently.

The priority was to find accommodation so I composed an advertisement to place in the Auckland Herald, with the office telephone number reading … 'young Englishman, recently arrived in Auckland seeks accommodation, preferably with a family.' Over three days, the switchboard fielded forty six replies and I had the calls fed in to dual lines, so that someone could locate the areas – Auckland is well spread. We reduced the possibilities to five but not after one woman immediately asked my age, to which I replied honestly, only to be told "oh dear, too young for me" that prompted a roar down the office "Get the number." A delightful family lived at the fifth visited possibility and as I was leaving to mull over the five, the wife told me that some years before, her husband, the chief chemist for a pharmaceutical company, had arrived from England, so she well appreciated my circumstances and even if I did not take up their offer, there was always a welcome. As I was leaving she gave me the family name – Gunton – my own; I stayed in this happy home throughout my time in New Zealand, 'my' name was in the telephone book straight away, (there were only two Guntons listed), and the husband's ancestors came from the same area in England as my own, the Fens, and on some occasions, we were judged to be very similar in appearance – a family link may be?

The principle responsibility of Tea and Coffee department was to buy tea for one of the Auckland food processing companies, who gave me free rein to import teas from any tea producing area, prepare blending sheets and never to exceed a landed Auckland docks cost of 3/11$^{1}/_{4}$d per pound. One month, due to world markets, I could not land below 4/0$^{1}/_{4}$d per pound but I managed to average down on the next shipment largely due to sourcing Carey Island tea from Malaysia. This tea, (now replaced by palm oil), was grown below sea level on land protected by a substantial bund, or bank, the liquor possessed no quality but it was ideally neutral and the leaf excellent, black, neat with reliable volume, so I had my blend reducer, approximately 10%. Two loose tea packets were involved and shipping opportunities to Auckland were regular, with only one shipment being a headache. Tea purchased in Cochin for transhipment in Singapore, was on-carried twice, to Hong Kong, so when it was eventually received it had to be blended carefully into several blends, not the one that was intended.

The department also serviced the tea packing companies throughout the Auckland area and their combined turnover was significant, New Zealand being one of the highest tea consumers in the World per capita. One evening a friend (ex Colombo) and I were invited to give a tea lecture to a worthy women's organisation, I working the slides whilst my friend spoke, opening his address, "well ladies, I have earned my living by spitting" (tea tasting) – a significant inrush of breath was heard throughout the hall. As I was packing up I overheard one lady comment to her companion ... "All very interesting, but I always use Tynan Tips" (one of my two blends) "for it goes down the sink so much easier." Market research should have taken note – my other blend was 'Digest' a bold leaf pekoe blend that would really have clogged up her plumbing.

After I had my feet under the desk I was asked to diversify, that was good value and one afternoon, I made my first sale to a farmer in the back sticks, (a really rural area) of a flame thrower with a lethal flame, that was strapped to my back, basically used to control gorse in paddocks. I also tried my hand at printed balloon sales, as the Company was agent for a rubber factory; the balloons were all different colours and one potential buyer requested all be blown up to admire the shades. I think that he was testing the pommie for he asked me to blow up additional ones (quite unnecessary) so the Pommie replied "you blow the next b….. lot up." Back came the prompt reply … "five hundred of each colour please" – one of the largest orders that Christmas.

I enjoyed the refreshing company of all the staff, they were a great bunch but I sailed close to the wind with our Director when I was requested to organize an office party. Afterwards, everyone congratulated me on the finest party that had ever been held but a month later a bellow rang out as the bill was received and I was asked to explain – "Well"– I advised "in Cochin consumption for office parties was calculated at half a bottle of spirits per head." "Not in New Zealand" came the reply – the 1800 hours closing law was in existence – but I retained my position as office steward.

My mother had retained an old family address in Whangarei, out of contact for over forty years, and suggested that I enquire if any relative could now be traced. Within a month of my arrival, I sat down to a family gathering of three generations who initially could not believe that I was a relative at 25 years old. They had all imagined a person of at least 60 years old, coming from India, but a whole new branch of the family was reunited and this link is now even more firmly established with the youngest backpacking generation journeying to us in Ireland. Sailing was a joy in Auckland and I made contact with the Royal New Zealand Yacht Squadron and was immediately accepted as a crew member of a K Class, racing keeler, one of twelve in her class, with a crew of five and an owner who was a construction engineer. He was a tough character who raced his boat and crew to the edge but he forged a good reliable

25

crew with mutual respect all round. I was invited to join the crew of the Ariki, my second season, a most beautiful gaffed rigged vessel built in 1905 with her own embossed cutlery and crockery and owned by two delightful characters. Each crew member had to be a different profession to deal with any problem afloat, a doctor, mechanic, tailor, electrician, carpenter – I looked after the stores, wet and dry, and we mustered ten all told, minimum seven, but this number was tight, particularly at night when I spent the Auckland / Kawau Island race at the base of the bowsprit, soaked, identifying smaller racing yachts that had started in earlier classes and that we were constantly overtaking in the spume. Non racing weekends were spent cruising the beautiful Hauraki Gulf and our home in England was later named Te Kouma Cottage (Maori for breast plate) after a haven on the Coromandel coast. On these occasions, all girl friends, partners and wives were more than welcome aboard for 'Cake Days' and on the morrow cruising back to Auckland, those with hangovers, were encouraged to take the Ariki pick-me-up, claret and lemonade – it worked wonders.

Cicely was able to visit New Zealand and arrived after my first year, working as a children's nurse, but we did have a glorious Easter 1966 touring South Island as far as Bluff, the Lands End, where we had the distinction of being ejected from a motor camp because we signed in with different surnames, unmarried. Earlier, we had become engaged in Pio Pio and despite the ring, the owner was unmoved. One evening, working our way up the west coast, we were lent an unfinished riverside cabin by the owner who also owned the completed one next door where, after supper with all of us together, a Maori arrived and sang to Cicely, beautifully, whilst sitting on his box of fresh oysters. The Haast Past road was opened that Easter weekend, only just, but we ploughed through waiting, on occasions, for bulldozers to clear the numerous rock and mud slides.

Great memories of a happy two years that were about to end with a posting back to London in November 1966 – Tea Department eight years on, what a change, but I also have the memory in New Zealand when my tea tasting palate was required for quality control of another liquor, Guinness. A director from Dublin was assessing bottles from St James's Gate against those just produced in New Zealand, before launching the local brew on the Market. At the end of the evening, every bottle tasted equally good so shipments from overseas, stopped forthwith!

"ARIRI"

AUCKLAND HARBOUR 1966

"ARIRI"

THE AUTHOR FAR LEFT

THE ROYAL NEW ZEALAND YACHT SQUADRON
ANNIVERSARY DAY REGATTA 1965

CREW MEMBER THELMA R3

THE ROYAL NEW ZEALAND YACHT SQUADRON
ANNIVERSARY DAY REGATTA 1966

'A' CLASS STARTING POSITIONS

RANGER - HINE MOA - JUPITOR - NORTHERNER - AROHIA
- TEAROA - ARIKI - MOANA

CREW MEMBER ARIKI A3

TWO'S COMPANY

On the 24th January 1967 Cicely and I were married by the Right Rev. Arthur Butler, Bishop of Tuam, Killala and Achonry at St Crumnathy's Cathedral, Achonry in Co Sligo, betwixt Tubbercurry and Ballinacarrow and our reception was held in her family home, Temple House, a beautiful setting in a beautiful part of the world and our Day was also blessed with sunny weather, frosty but almost cloudless. We spent our honeymoon partly in Ireland and partly around Exmoor where one evening we stayed in an old pub at Porlock Weir. The landlord, ex Argentine Railways, gave us a warm welcome and his bar had been fitted with London underground hand straps from the oak beam – one could literally hang on after a pint or two.

We established our home in a spacious country home in Brasted, Kent, a first floor flat with a spiral outside staircase to the garden. I had no idea where to start looking for accommodation after two years in New Zealand so I placed an advertisement in the personal column of The Times. Nine replies were received one of which was from a retired Air Marshall who had seen our advertisement whilst on holiday with his wife in Madeira – 'country loving newly weds seek accommodation near London.' We were invited to tea one Saturday in December and as I absorbed the atmosphere, my eyes fell upon four carved penguins on the mantelpiece. I had seen those penguins before at my prep school carved by their son from whale's teeth when he was working on a whaling ship in the South Atlantic before teaching me geography when I was ten years old, and before marrying the headmaster's youngest daughter. He later followed a career in the Army and founded the Exeter maritime museum in retirement.

Meadowgate was a happy home and our landlord was then the Chairman of the British Spiritualists Society who became well known after writing a book entitled 'The Night My Number Came Up,' a personal experience in the Far East during WWII. He established a bothy at the top of the garden approached through a sweep of daffodils in the spring where he held sessions, communicating with people who had departed this life. He was a lovable character and early one frosty morning I stood in amazement as he padded around the garden in dressing gown and slippers, placing long wooden clothes pegs into the lawn. His hot bathwater had melted the frost immediately above the drainage pipes and for a magical few minutes he was able to identify the pipe layout exactly. Near the garage stood a lime tree, still alive after being straffed by machinegun fire during a war time dog fight over Kent and within ten miles of Biggin Hill. Despite retirement he was invited to take a March Past there when his wife was away, so Cicely's rather regal grandmother, who was staying with us, stepped into the breach and they made a fine pair on the dais. After the proceedings we were given a tour of the base, including the chapel, where one of the stained glass windows incorporates a Mosquito, (insect) to remember those aircraft based there during the war.

I commuted daily to the office, bus to Sevenoaks station and into Cannon Street but the tea trade was facing changing times and the tea auction venue in Mincing Lane, offering North Indian teas for sale on Mondays, Ceylon and South Indian teas on Tuesdays and African teas on Wednesdays – moved to the new 'Centre for the Tea Trade' in Upper Thames Street. The old auction room was a fine venue though, occupying a seventh and eighth floor with no ceiling / floor between them, so the room was a lofty and spacious auditorium. I was alerted that the sixteen tea producing country shields approximately 4ft x 4ft, four of which adorned each wall, were being scrapped, so I made my number with the building contractor, drove up to the City the very next Saturday and obtained four that are now restored and on loan to the Tea Museum near Southwark Cathedral.

There was a distinct reduction in Tea Brokers ... Some of the first hand brokers who printed their own weekly tea catalogues, basically the auctioneers, had amalgamated but several of the second hand brokers had disappeared. These gentlemen were the real traders who often worked from one or two rooms, in places such as Seething Lane, Rood Lane and Idle Lane where there was one extremely knowledgeable gentleman who only traded in China teas. I was fortunate to have glimpsed this fascinating significant part of the Tea Trade, now long gone.

We had one particularly interesting task a few weeks after the 1967 Middle East war, when a convoy of ships was trapped in the Suez Canal for months, two of which were carrying Ceylon teas consigned to the London Auctions. The company had over 2,000 tea chests aboard the Blue Funnel vessel, Melampus, and whilst general average was declared by the insurance assessers they were eventually allowed aboard the vessels to draw samples for the consignees to taste and value. We liquored the two batches and the leaf had become much blacker, also the infusions much duller than average but the liquors whilst flat, were not nearly as unpalatable as anticipated. We later discovered that 'our' teas had been stowed below the ship's water line – above it, the teas would have been baked and probably undrinkable. History does not relate what happened to the tea once discharged but ironically, with a much improved blacker leaf appearance, demanded by the Middle East, there was a ready market on the dockside.

Our son Malcolm arrived on All Saints Day 1967, and sitting in an ante room at Sevenoaks Hospital, with two other expectant Dads, one exclaimed that it was fourth time around for him and that his wife had better hurry up as his morning milk round was due to commence at 0400 hrs. Cicely was a quick operator and had asked me to be present but the midwife was short and sweet as I donned a white tunic and mask. I was reminded that I had attended none of the talks for expectant dads and if I fainted, I would be left on the floor. We soon rejoiced at the arrival of our first born son and the doctor patted me on the back and congratulated me, apparently thinking that I was the stand-by anaesthetist, and left. We had never met him before, he had been summoned as our own doctor was away, but in fact, he was Sir Winston Churchill's country doctor from nearby Westerham.

Shortly afterwards, I received an alert that we were due to move to Sri Lanka early in the New Year, so we spent Christmas in Cornwall and then visited Ireland where our son was christened Malcolm Tristan Robert, with his mother, grandmother and great grandmother in attendance.

2427 (BIGGIN HILL) SQUADRON
AIR TRAINING CORPS

SUNDAY 21st MAY, 1967

A parade to mark the official
opening of the Squadron's
new headquarters.

Guests are kindly requested to
be seated by 10.50 hours.

Cars may be parked between the
two hangars.

THE BIGGIN HILL MARCH PAST PROGRAMME

SHIELDS OF FOUR TEA PRODUCING NATIONS
ON LOAN TO THE TEA MUSEUM, LONDON

SERENDIB

A return to the tropics in early 1968 was really welcome after a year of commuting and the Company provided us with an apartment in Baurs flats, in Chatham Street, five minutes walk from the office in Prince Building, Prince Street, Fort Colombo. The Company was a first class operation in the capital city for in addition to the Tea department, there were Shipping, Insurance, Estates and Accounts departments, whilst at Darley Road a large warehouse complex with wharves beside the Beira Lake also accommodated a Printing and Tea Chest Components department, where skilled carpenters could knock up chests in under two minutes. Elsewhere in town, an engineering complex and boat building yard flourished.

Tea department was a major tea exporter achieving a turnover of up to one million pounds some weeks, with the major account situated in Durban. Other main accounts were Iraq and Iran, (we had one or two Iranians with us for several months each year), Australia, New Zealand, Canada, America, Holland, Pakistan and later on, England. Smaller accounts included the Vatican City (we also printed their distinctive packets), Chile, Afghanistan (when shipments had to be packed in special size, flatter chests covered in gunny, for transport at destination on yaks). Other small accounts included Malta, the Faroes and the Falkland Islands, Iceland, Germany, Italy and several other countries – we were always hungry for business. Like Cochin, the department also had the responsibility of handling teas from the tea estates administered by the Company as managing agents, plus a few tea estates still in private ownership.

Blending tea was a major part of the company business, the blend components being original teas, manufactured by individual tea estates and bought in the weekly tea auctions. The buyers prepared their own standards of tea to suit their local market, samples of which they sent to Colombo for matching and once approved, prices and availability were relayed to them every week with orders being placed when prices and quality were considered attractive. Some of these blends totalled several hundred tea chests, equally divided into mixes to be accommodated in the 2,000 or 5,000 pound revolving blending drums. However for the Orange Pekoe blends, comprising long wiry leaf the 'Umbrella' blending method was used, pouring the leaf onto the top of a steel shade that then flowed down the sides to a circle below, thus preventing the leaf from fragmenting. Repacking tea sometimes created problems afterwards: we had a complaint one year from New York that a rat had been found in one of the chests and checking records we found that the tea had been packed in the Monsoon and the rat had, probably, run in to the dry warehouse and then found an even more acceptable refuge in the chest. All was forgiven but the rat became quite famous, being sent to the Smithsonian Institute for identification – a 'ratus ratus' no less of Asian origin. The Calcutta office had a similar experience with frogs at destination but the manager saved the day, and probably the account, by heading the apology letter 'Dessicated Amphibians'.

Whilst I became heavily involved in tea, Cicely and Malcolm were soon absorbed in to the young social group and there was a happy welcoming number of expatriates and Ceylonese families in town. The Colombo Hockey and Football Club – CH and FC - was our main watering hole, the Colombo Swimming Club – CSC a close second – whilst we later joined the Royal Colombo Yacht Club in Colombo port, the Ceylon Motor Yacht Club, sited out of town on the Bolgoda Lake, where I was a member of the Ceylon sailing team against India one year, the Darawella Sailing Club in the hills, surrounded by tea estates, and the Ceylon Sea

Anglers Club, the old RAF mess in Trincomalee. Several trophies came our way, including the ladies cup won by Cicely at Bolgoda, that gave me great pleasure one season, and en route to Darawella for a regatta, we drove through a tropical downpour with our Enterprise in tow that filled up with water, to such an extent that I had to stop and bail her out, the extra weight being too much for our Morris 1000 Traveller.

The Darawella Sailing Club was surrounded by rolling tea clad hills and on one estate, three young expatriate planters shared a bungalow. They observed that the sherry decanter continually showed lower levels despite the fact that their main alcoholic intake was beer. The cook and houseboy were approached but both were quite adamant that neither of them was tippling but the level continued to drop, so they took the decision to pee in the decanter and re-establish a healthy level. The next evening the level had dropped again the staff were summoned and the cook confessed, "Ah master, I am taking one tablespoon every evening to add to your soup." It was wise, though to keep an eye on alcohol and a friend of ours had a nudge when he lost his keys to his supplies stored in a carved chest, at sundowner time. The head bearer and assistant came in, both took a handle at each end and bodily lifted the four sides, with the locked lid attached, off the base, revealing all bottles twinkling. Our friend had kept his stock religiously locked for years.

Sailing weekends at Trincomalee were special though, one of the largest natural harbours in the world, ringed by sandy beaches … Sweat Bay … Marble Bay … but the journey took us through several jungle areas. Cicely exclaimed at dusk one time … "careful elephant" … "nonsense" I replied to quell her anxiety … "tree trunks" … but two bends later on the narrow road there were indeed eight grey tree trunks ambling along with two twitching tails, the rear view of two adult elephants. The Ceylon Sea Anglers Club had many non paying members, monkeys, that swung from roof to roof snatching anything that took their fancy and causing fear and alarm one night when one went to sleep on top of a loo cistern in the Ladies, the tail hanging down and judged (in panic), to be a snake.

We had moved to a house in Queens Road just before the insurgency in 1971 where we lived with a curfew for eight months, not easy, and initially with only four hours freedom, after the first two days with none at all. Three families and two bachelors became organised and every two days we moved to a different house for company and a change of scene, dogs, too, and often with some of our house staff, glad to have some reliable company. However, our cook took to the bottle one night, not the first time, but certainly more heavily than before and whilst the men were having a quick sail at the Royal Colombo Yacht Club, Cicely telephoned the police and asked if they could please come and remove our prone servant from the residence. Cicely and her friends had a ringside seat as her telephone call caused immediate reaction from the security forces thinking that we had a prone insurgent. The servants quarters were virtually stormed, the cook departed, prone, feet first, and I called into the police station homeward bound to assess the situation. "No problem" I was told … "curfew is at 1800 hrs tonight and we shall let him out at 1801 hrs." I persuaded the authorities to hold him overnight and a very sheepish, hungover cook returned in the morning. It was a great credit to the tea trade though, that throughout the curfew period no tea auction was cancelled; the tea was driven from the estates to Colombo in convoys obeying the curfew hours and shipments continued.

It was in Queens Road, though, that we experienced our only burglary – Cicely's bag on her side of the bed was rifled for the house keys in the early hours whilst we were asleep and it was probably as well that neither of us woke up. It was in this bed, too, that I used to read in the evening before turning the light off, book in one hand, squash racquet in the other, zapping the cockroaches as they flew through the large open window – high flyers in Colombo, the bedroom was on the first floor.

One Saturday morning, a thoughtful snake charmer appeared for the children's benefit, sat himself down, crossed legged opposite the front door and beside the potted plants and began to play merrily upon his flute. Awakened the cobra obligingly slid out of the basket observed the cool lush surroundings and shot down the nearest drain. No amount of frantic fluting could tempt the cobra to return, so we retreated to the swimming club but returning later, we were assured that the reptile had been safely retrieved.

Labour problems rumbled from time to time and we had a major strike one year when the executive staff doubled up to do what was necessary. I spent time being driven around the mercantile area, collecting teas from different warehouses that the company had purchased in auction, in a mechanical horse, a three wheeled cab with a detachable trailer. I held the record, collecting 133 tea chests on one trip that started off dramatically, the cab reared up with the front wheel two feet off the ground but a redistribution of tea chests and weight, solved the problem.

We also experienced the introduction of the poya calendar, based entirely on the phases of the moon that caused so many problems with our customers overseas that we printed a special company calendar for their benefit. Eight day weeks and Tuesday / Wednesday, or Thursday / Friday weekends, depending on the moon, were difficult to explain to some folk.

At a cocktail party early one evening, Cicely was asked if I would be prepared to model some clothes being presented the following evening at sunset by a fashion house in Colombo, at the Mount Lavinia Hotel. 'Ask him later' the designer was advised, which she did and I apparently accepted with pleasure – a fact that I was joyfully reminded of early the following morning. The usual male model was away and we drove along to the venue at dusk to view a T shaped stage under the floodlit palm trees, with the surf breaking on the beach beyond. The two male models were asked to escort the four girls in turn, all of us displaying the beautiful batik clothing that the fashion house had produced and they had advertised well attracting a very large audience, including many tourists. The show was hugely successful and I was invited to accept any one of the garments that I had modelled. I chose a unique smoking jacket that I have to this day. Another modelling evening was held two months later in a Colombo house – equally successful – but I have never catwalked since!

On a more serious note, a summons was received one day to report for jury service at the High Court, an unusual honour for any expatriate and unheard of to be called for service a second time, but I was, less than two years later and on that occasion acting as foreman. Both cases were murder trials and both the accused had opted to have an English speaking jury, in the belief that they would receive a fairer trial, despite the fact that neither could speak English themselves. The evidence did not ring true, in either trial – we found both 'Not Guilty'. In all the time that I spent at the courts I never saw another expatriate and interestingly enough, at the first trial, H.M. the Queen's photograph was displayed above the judge, at the second trial a photograph of the president Mrs S Bandaranike had been hung instead, as the Country had meantime become a Republic.

Our last long journey was to Jaffna and we had a reminder of the Curfew two years before, driving along the main road northwards, on sand, and in remote territory. Cicely was wearing a bikini, I was wearing a pair of swimming trunks and Malcolm aged five was in the back of our Morris 1000 Traveller. We drove round a corner to see a bamboo pole completely across the road at bonnet height, and as soon as we had stopped two uniformed armed men appeared on each side of the vehicle. I got out immediately and offered my open palm, that both men shook pointing with their rifles at the rear doors. The vehicle and the luggage were thoroughly searched before the bamboo barrier was pulled up and we were waved on, none the wiser.

Our lasting family link, though, was the birth of our second son, Seamus Douglas Tara who arrived at the Joseph Frazer Nursing Home on the 3rd January 1971. Aged two, he was to move to his father's birthplace, England: there had been a resignation in head office and I was to return to my old tasting counter in London – again – in 1973.

Great memories we retain of those five years, including .....
    "Let your arm pits be your charm pits
    Use Odour −o − no"
Radio Ceylon advertisement.

    "All the water in this Hotel has been passed,
    Personally by the Manager"
Notice in Gall Face Hotel foyer.

"The bride looked quite beautiful as she emerged from the Church attended by six bridesmaids and the Groom very handsome is his morning suit with a red carnation in his bottom hole."
Social column of a national daily newspaper.

HANNA AND PAUL

MARIPOSA FASHION SHOW   MOUNT LAVINIA HOTEL

PAUL HANNA URSULA CHANTI SUSAN PETER

DOLDRUM YEARS

There was really no full time job for an assistant manager in the London tea department by that time, for the trade had shrunk further, there had been more amalgamations, many second hand brokers no longer existed and the London tea auctions had shrunk to one and a half days per week. However, there was a variety of work, including trading on the London coffee futures market, a completely different animal to the conservative, traditional tea trade as the Company had recently acquired coffee interests in New Guinea. I shared an office with a genial manager, ex Colombo tea department, who consumed over thirty full strength Capstan cigarettes a day – during working hours – so looking back it was remarkable that I did not suffer from passive smoking effects. However, becoming a member of the tea trade packaging sub committee at its conception, was an interesting diversion, tea chests were becoming less used and one of the committee's briefs was to visit UK ports to examine the condition of newly introduced paper sacks on arrival, now almost universally adopted for palletized, containerised shipments. I also enjoyed one 'jolly' representing the UK Tea Buyers Association at a UK Traffic Day hosted by the port of Antwerp. Never to be forgotten were the annual sailing days, the compliments of a leading London warehouse company who entertained their clients on a Thames sailing barge, the Cabby, sailing from the Medway into the

Thames estuary to return, often with a weather beaten complement in the evening – no reflection on the sea conditions though.

I commuted in to Liverpool Street station as Cicely and I had decided to find a home in Essex and initially, we rented a house in Witham where I willingly agreed to manage the garden. I was clearing out the garden shed and found a photograph of a tea planting club in Ceylon, taken in the 1930's with the members grouped outside. The previous owner had lived in Ceylon and we had known her son who worked for one of the plantation companies. However, we found our new home, three miles away in Hatfield Peverel that remains in the family. The second owner was a retired tea planter from North India and we bought from a family emigrating to Australia, a country that we both visited en route to New Zealand.

We moved in and awaited our baggage from Colombo, packed into one huge wooden crate weighing over a ton. The packers had built a rectangle of all items in the largest room of our spacious home, took measurements and then built the wooden crate in the garden, exactly to size on the lawn, and then set to work packing the contents. The final weight almost defeated the mobile crane, the rear wheels rising significantly off the lawn but away it went to reappear in Glebefield Road. We needed a similar machine to lift the crate from the hauliers lorry but the local dairy obliged with a fork lift and when I came to settle their account, I was advised "No charge, welcome to the village." It is a testimony to the original carpenters, and their choice of timber, that the crate is still very much in existence, as a garden shed.

We enjoyed those years in the village, the boys attended the school down the road, I became chairman of the Parent Teachers Association for two years, a member of the Parish Council and we all joined the nearby Blackwater Sailing Club (I still remain a member) and we entered our firefly, *Schnell* F2129, in the Silver Jubilee tideway race from Putney to the Tower of London, with Cicely and the boys photographing progress from several of the London bridges – quite a day in 1977. There were, however, two great 'windows' in this period, a return to Cochin in 1976 and to Mombasa in 1978, to manage the respective tea departments

SILVER JUBILEE TIDEWAY RACE   9TH JULY 1977
'SCHNELL'   FIREFLY F2129

BEFORE THE START OF THE RETURN RACE TO PUTNEY
(UPRIVER ON THE FLOOD TIDE)

whilst the local managers took annual furloughs but this time on my own.

Several changes had taken place when Cicely, Malcolm and I had visited Cochin in 1968 on a similar temporary secondment but it was wonderful for me to share the place in 1968, and memories, with the family – also, for Cicely who had last visited Cochin as a child when her father was tea planting in the nearby High Range. We took the opportunity to visit her old home on Chittavurrai Estate and when we walked along the main corridor, I tapped a door and said it opened into the bedroom that I slept in as a bachelor when staying with a friend who was the then manager. The same bedroom was Cicely's as a little girl, years before we met in Ireland – a room with a fire at night, necessary at an altitude of almost 7,000ft and where I first lay in bed watching the shadows of firelight flickering on a ceiling. My billiard cue was still hanging on the rack in the Cochin club and was retrieved and taken back to Colombo, with a rosewood cot specially made for Malcolm in the High Range and on his first birthday he took his first steps and old, loyal, Annie arrived at the front door with a basket of fruit for little master and went home with a suitable token of real gratitude.

We stayed in two houses during that visit, one near the Dobhi Ghats, washing areas, and also inhabited by hundreds of frogs. They were in the drive to welcome us at night, gathered on the front door step, in the hall, hopped up the stairs with us, were in the air conditioned bedroom, peering over the curtain rail as we drew the curtains and some variety of frog even walked across the ceiling, upside down – now, Cicely cannot tolerate frogs, anywhere. Our second house was immediately opposite, and behind, the Naval shore battery who were kind enough to alert us when their next firing practice would be conducted to a towed target, offshore. We were advised by our neighbours to take all pictures off the walls and secure all ornaments, which I thought were rather extreme measures, but one lunchtime, our tranquillity was shattered by a series of shells being fired. The house shook to its foundations, all unsecured items danced around and I drew blood inside my mouth with the prongs of a fork whilst I was poised eating.

It was during this first secondment that I spent, probably, my most enjoyable business day ever. The Coonoor tea auctions had started, catering for tea producers who wished to sell mainly secondary grades locally – rather than truck them down to Cochin, two hundred miles away. Armed with orders, one from Vancouver, Cicely, Malcolm and I stayed on Terramia estate and I drove in early, through beautiful tea clad hills to be in attendance at 0900 hrs. The auctions were held on Saturdays in the men's bar of the Coonoor club, the auctioneer conducting proceedings behind the bar with all the buyers on stools or chairs. I secured my quantities below prices that the overseas buyers were prepared to pay, the tea market being easier that morning, cross checked purchases with the brokers to ensure prices, quantities and tea details were absolutely correct before the brokers issued their contracts and then walked along the lane to join the family and our host for a curry lunch in a beautiful bungalow garden. Interestingly enough, two weeks later, I was asked to report to the customs who suspected a case of under invoicing but evidence that all the teas involved in the Canadian shipment were secondary grades ex Coonoor, satisfied the authorities – no such teas were available at similar prices in the Cochin auctions.

After lunch we visited the Ootacamund club and up swept a really colourful Standard Vanguard as her paintwork had worn down to different shades after years baking in the sun. At the wheel was the character Queenie Wapshire, a classic case of "staying on" who had come for her weekly bridge afternoon. Some months before during the session, a bearer had presented a note to Queenie, on a silver tray, advising that the ceiling in one of her principal rooms had collapsed: Queenie played on. The Ooty club is remembered for being the place where Winston Churchill was refused membership and where snooker was invented but not for the 1920's incident, when an elderly expatriate military man tripped over a prone couple on the lawn one evening and was heard to mutter in the bar later, "Damn it, he wasn't even a member."

By 1976, the expatriate population had reduced to three people, replaced by competent, disciplined really welcoming Indian managers. Several times during the three months on my own, I insisted on evenings alone staying at home in another bungalow behind the shore Battery – I could not keep up the social pace, that included the delightful wife of a tea broker who was a national pop idol. I still have her records, she was blessed with a beautiful and stunning voice. The chummery was empty, the walls holding many stories, unable to be told; I climbed over the front gate and found a Portuguese gravestone in the undergrowth, well etched with a family shield, that had been unearthed in my bachelor days whilst a vegetable garden was being established. Permission was granted for me to remove this stone for safe keeping, so I organised a gang of willing helpers with a hand cart and we delivered it to St Francis Church – just as well for the chummery has since been demolished and the site redeveloped – a little piece of Malabar coast history had been saved though. The gravestone has since been placed on a stone slab just inside the Church on the right hand side.

During the Easter weekend, I made a nostalgic visit to Munnar where in the men's bar of the High Range Club there is a wonderful display of ex tea planters' hats. These tea planters had served not less than thirty years in the District and were identified by their initials and years of service. I spent a day trekking over the grass hills with a guide and resting in a village thatched hut, provided with a mat and a glass of honey. Another day, I climbed Anai Mudi, the highest peak in India south of the Himalayas at 8,841 ft and admired the spectacular view including the High Range planting district on one side, the Anamallai tea district on the other. On our descent, we had to lie up for a good half hour, heads above the long grass, whilst a herd of elephants grazed across our path, less than a hundred yards distant. 'The sturdy scale' – a guide to judge trout aplenty in the district – signed by my father-in-law over twenty years earlier – still hung in a fishing hut and a wonderful bonus was to discover my old canoe, *Petronella*, in a tea estate garage. The Indian Navy agreed to refurbish her in the Cochin Naval Base workshops – I had been a member of their United Services Officers Club earlier – Clan Line agreed to ship her to Avonmouth as a parcel (free) and she is still in good order in Ireland.

I enjoyed my secondment to Mombasa in 1978 where the weekly tea auctions were conducted and where, basically the company business was purchasing tea in the auctions, blending a very large proportion of the purchases before shipment, similar to the operation in Cochin and Colombo but without direct involvement with the tea estates. After three months resident in Mombasa Club, I returned home just before Christmas and on my first evening Cicely asked me to bring in some coal. Initially I could not understand why I was not making much progress; the heap was frozen together. Later when Cicely came into our bedroom I heard the words "pick – up – your – clothes -." I cocked an eye and had to admit that a pair of trousers were in one place, a shirt in another, a pullover somewhere else – room 23 in the Mombasa Club, above the men's bar, was a fading memory, and so too was Joseph the loyal room servant who had tended faithfully to all my foibles.

Little did I realize, though, that the three months in Mombasa were a prelude of events to come. The manager for whom I had acted, resigned early in the New Year, and I was appointed manager of the operation and flew out to take up the permanent position in May 1979.

LIFE ON THE COAST

The three month secondment had stood me in good stead, as I knew the establishment of the business well in Mombasa but it was certainly different from Cochin and Colombo tea departments. Firstly the staff numbered only seven, with myself the only tea taster and secondly, we did not have our own warehouses, all that side of the business being conducted, on contract, by one of the specialised handling agents. Also, as the tea estates were established beyond Nairobi, we visited the districts only occasionally but they were beautiful, notably Kericho and the Nandi Hills. Our buyers were many, often the same ones to whom I had shipped teas previously, but shipping had improved considerably with pallets and containers and Mombasa, of course, was served by numerous shipping lines. It was often worthwhile for shippers, though, to shop around for freight rates; for example, to ship tea to Vancouver, via Antwerp, Halifax and land bridge to destination, was cheaper and quicker than opportunities direct, via the Panama Canal. The buying and blending prospered, the latter orders being executed on an exclusive parquet floor area in our agent's complex, but it was essential to make very regular visits. All containers were professionally inspected by a third party prior to stuffing, and a certificate issued accordingly, but arriving one day when the doors of one container were being closed, I noticed one tea chest had been patched. There was no time to repack the tea, so I had the pallet turned around – first impressions, on arrival, were important.

Our main account was in England and we welcomed their blenders regularly whilst Pakistan was an important outlet. I paid a business visit one year to Karachi, and walking through the Bazaar, I do not think that I have ever been so hot, anywhere. Also I took our agents advice to keep one hand on my head to stop camels seizing my hair and the final evening I was persuaded to take a beach ride on one of those animals. The next day, I spent the entire flight to Kenya sitting on the edge of my seat, the camel saddle had rubbed my coccyx severely! A mention in the annual Company head office report to shareholders highlighted improved annual tea turnover in Mombasa, that was a fillip, but competition remained strong and every order, large and small, was significant. Each working week ended on a Saturday, when traditionally all the tea buyers gathered at De Souza's bar, near the docks entrance, before going home for lunch. One year a De Souza's tie was created in London for all the patrons but the ties were only available to those people who had bought a round, and from time to time I still wear mine with some nostalgia.

Initially, we lived at Likoni south of Mombasa harbour, sometimes waiting a long time for the ferry onto Mombasa Island and off the other side, over, apparently the longest floating bridge in the world, when we were travelling north – so we moved to Nyali. We employed a series of watchmen, the family favourite being one Dismas Otwani, tall, quiet and very serious. We always shared our Christmas meal with the staff and Seamus took out a cracker on one occasion to share with Dismas who had never set eyes on one before. The cracker went 'bang' and I do not think that he had ever had such a fright in his life but he wore his paper hat every night, on duty, until it finally disintegrated just before Easter. He was prone to snoozing whilst on duty and often I did not have the heart to wake him as he always looked so peaceful but one morning I took him to task: he explained that he was not asleep during the night only resting deeply (very). However the day came when a warning letter was necessary, (three such letters resulted in dismissal), but it was all rather a pointless exercise and the exchange ran along the following lines …

"Dismas, I have a letter for you"

"Oh Bwana thank you, thank you."

"No Dismas! - this is a warning letter."

"Oh, a letter from Bwana and signed, thank you, thank you."

"No Dismas this – is – a – warning – letter"

"Oh Bwana thank you, thank you."

I gave up, not something I have done very often. Game, set and match to Dismas, and I found a good job for him when we finally left Kenya, as a watchman at a tea warehouse.

Also, it was the garden boy's duty to top up the bird bath with water in time for the dawn chorus, but there was a period when the bird bath was always empty when I came to breakfast at 0700 hrs – despite the garden boy's assurance that the job had been done – until I came on the scene earlier than usual one morning. Lying in the birdbath was a monkey idly splashing water over himself – bliss. We had snakes around too, they loved the dry coral garden walls, and if one in the garage was not bad enough when Seamus and I took out the table tennis table, a long one fell out of the thatched roof of our verandah whilst we were enjoying coffee after dinner. It landed with a thud and we placed our feet on the table under which it slithered, down the steps and away into the garden. The staff later told us that it had lived in the cool of the roof before we had even moved to the property, 27 Jamhuri Road, a memorable family home.

We had shipped our Albacore sailing dinghy from the Blackwater Sailing Club, that gave us much pleasure, and she was based at the Mombasa Sailing Club where I was Rear Commodore at one stage. Cicely, too became a fine windsurfer with the boys and we sailed in some other beautiful settings including Lake Naivasha. At one regatta, all competitors had launched, but before the five minute signal was given, seven hippo surfaced on the starting line and the race was postponed for fifteen minutes.

Cicely purchased a large framed tent shortly after our arrival that we used extensively, one year opting out of leave to England to explore northern Kenya – a great investment. On our way south we tarried at the Masai Mara to see the wildebeest migration, pitching the tent for three nights on the banks of a river, within a camping area. On the opposite side was a ranger's hut and up to one million wildebeest as far as the eye could see. The first evening at sunset we had company, a Masai standing beside me, spear in left hand, right foot against his left knee and with no movement. After half an hour, Cicely enquired if there were 'five for dinner.' I rose from beside the camp fire, he and I shook hands, bowed and I presented two empty beer bottles as a gift that he would find very useful, after which he faded into the night. We never saw him again but someone did enter our tent and finished the biscuits when we were game viewing the next day.

Many times we visited Lake Jipe, facing Tanzania on the opposite shore, with a magnificent view of Kilimanjaro, in fact, we spent four nights one Christmas in camp, playing snapdragon on Christmas Eve with fellow campers and Cicely cooking our turkey over the camp fire, in foil, the finest turkey that we have ever enjoyed. The tent was bedecked with decorations and on Boxing Day, a party of American tourists passed by and offered us accommodation at Taita Hills Lodge (Hilton Group) nearby – they could not believe that we had been in residence for three nights already. An American tea buyer also expressed astonishment at our Loo – a sentry box, one hundred yards from the campsite but commanding a magnificent view across Tsavo Game Park West and with the door open it was well worth taking a pair of binoculars for observing game whilst on the throne but not so good at night in the darkness. I had to make a journey once, on foot but doubled back smartly to collect the car after a call from a nearby lion, but leaving the door open with the headlights on to give some light, I soon became smothered in insects. However, the American just had to photograph our facilities, otherwise his fiancée in New York would not believe his exposure to such conditions, and he sent us a photograph of our camp fire, that is now framed and on our kitchen wall in Ireland.

Near Lake Jipe is the WWI battle site of Salita Hill that at one stage was occupied by the German forces from neighbouring Tanganyika. One can still walk along the trenches that ring the Hill and find evidence of the two battles that took place in 1916. It is an interesting place to roam and to visit the British War Graves Cemeteries in nearby Taveta, and Voi where one Victoria Cross holder is buried. One morning, I picked up a shell that was later to be defused by the bomb disposal team aboard the aircraft carrier USS America, the leader stating that it was a unique exercise and the subject that would open his lectures, once he took up a shore appointment later in the year. On my part I sent details of all markings and an outline to the Imperial War Museum in London – not only was the shell identified but also, the day on which it was fired in 1916 and it is now in my study in Ireland. I later telephoned the gentleman in London to express my thanks that he heartily reciprocated, explaining that for years he only had the daily commute but my letter had allowed him to enjoy three days of 'delicious researching' amongst the archives.

One unexpected and very welcoming period was when the Royal Navy used Mombasa and Kenya as recreational areas with regular visits of two weeks duration. Ships from the Royal Australian Navy and Royal New Zealand Navy also paid similar visits.

The Navies were generous with their hospitality and often the ships gave welcoming parties soon after arrival in port, organised by their resident officer in Mombasa, to introduce the ship's company to the residents and expatriates. One purser approached me to enquire where he could find tea to replace the NAFFI brew aboard, so the next day I drove to the quayside with three tea chests of office sample tea – no more than a month old ex-estate. Less than six months later, the agitated resident RN liaison officer appeared in my office to enquire how on earth my name was on the Admiralty NAFFI list as a ship's supplier of tea. All rather simple to explain but I think that he was a little miffed that his intelligence network had come adrift.

The resident RN liaison officer was a close neighbour and we offered our home and garden as a quiet haven for the ships' crews, an offer that was gratefully accepted. We enjoyed the company of numerous visitors, including a later First Sea Lord, and a few remain in Christmas contact each year. Several ships' crests in the house remind us of those days including the crest of HMS *Sheffield*, lost in the Falklands War a few weeks after she had sailed from Mombasa. A year later, we met the widow of one officer who was killed, who we remember as a charming character and a visitor to our home. She had joined him in Mombasa for his two weeks in port and said that if there had to be a swansong in their marriage, what better place than Mombasa.

The annual Kenya Safari Rally took our time annually after an approach by the coast organiser who admitted, that looking for assistance, he had spied Cicely and me on the Mombasa Club dance floor one evening and thought 'there's a reliable couple.' We were hooked and always opted for the most far flung, remote check points in Tsavo East and West manned by day and by night. This involvement led me to being navigator in a section route car, thundering through the bush, ensuring that the route was clear for the cars following three hours behind. On one daylight section, the Range Rover broke down after backfiring for a hundred yards and whilst the driver successfully effected repairs, I looked around and there was not a soul in sight, but there was a solitary giraffe peering around a nearby tree, curious to learn what on earth had disturbed the tranquillity. Little did he know there was far worse to come. I also navigated a car in the Mombasa Motor Club, Kasigau 300 Rally and became a member of the Institute of Advanced Motorists, Kenya to add to my membership of the Institute of Advanced Motorists, New Zealand Inc. The instructor in Auckland had ended the Test with the comment that it was obvious that I had not learnt to drive in New Zealand, a comment I relayed to the lads in the office, who put me in Coventry for two days, but there was no such comment in Mombasa.

Our boys had done well at their schools, the Mombasa Academy and Pembroke House in Gilgil but in 1983, all was about to change dramatically – I was made redundant, basically as the Company could not afford an expatriate in Mombasa with all the financial trimmings including two children at boarding school. By that time, there was no desk for me in tea department London, where business was slower, there were more reductions in the trade and the London Tea Auctions had reduced to one day per week. Also, what I did not know at the time was that there were big changes afoot for the Harrisons and Crosfield group, so if the change had to come, it was as well that it came when it did. We packed up our goods, the Albacore, too, that I could not sell and as luck would have it, a Tilbury bound container ship had sixteen empty units on board and Aquarius was accommodated in one, free of charge. We were homeward bound.

BACK TO BASE

O ur family home in Hatfield Peverel was awaiting our return and what a blessing – so many people we met in our travels did not have a property outside the country where they were employed, unwise, particularly in politically unstable nations. However, there was a company mortgage on the property, so I had to source a different provider and the Halifax Building Society came to our assistance, promptly, efficiently and willingly. Aquarius and our luggage were discharged at Tilbury and she came home within a week but the luggage was shipped LCL (less than a container load) and had to be destuffed and inspected by customs, along with everything else in the container, a process that took over three weeks – not popular on the home front. However, we were soon established and the neighbours gave us a warm welcome, also the church, shops, post office, the Cross Keys public house, garage and the sailing club where Aquarius was re-established and where I was re-elected to the committee, and three years later was elected Chairman of the Village Community Association.

I was not out of work for a day as a long standing friend, who had been in the same position as me, had started his own tea business, supported by his able wife. These two souls taught me a great deal about business in the UK in a very short time, often in a tense atmosphere created by increasing turnover - one week we purchased over 2,000 tea packages in the London Auctions, by that time a very significant percentage of the whole auction that was then being concluded well within a day – we all went out to the theatre to celebrate, seven staff and Cicely, followed by dinner in a restaurant.

The office was situated in the basement of Drayton House, opposite Euston Station and our major responsibility was the buying and blending for a notable company in Harrogate. Yorkshire water was brought from Harrogate each week for tasting teas and evaluation and all purchases on their behalf were allocated either to Yorkshire teabag east blends or Yorkshire teabag west blends, depending on the soft or hard water areas where the blends would be marketed - a successful strategy. I did not know Yorkshire but I was impressed with my first visit to Harrogate. On arrival at the station I asked the way to my hotel and realizing my situation, the person I asked, collected his car and delivered me to the doorstep. The crocus beds in the early morning were magnificent and the crisp air exhilarating in April.

Other major accounts included companies in Basingstoke and Woolwich but we were hungry for business, trading teas continually and producing smaller packets such as Lifeboat tea, a one off Earl Grey tea bag order for British Airways, and other Earl Grey orders. A Swiss account took the strongest scented bergamot, we bought the scent from a merchant who obtained it in Corsica and executed the blends in a warehouse opposite the Tower Hotel, in an area now completely redeveloped. I had been advised that the foreman was difficult to approach if he did not take to you, so on my first visit after the blending programme had been discussed, I suggested a pint at lunchtime. We retired to 'The Ship Aground,' discussed the world and worked happily together thereafter. We tendered for one Admiralty tea contract with delivery to four different Naval Bases in the United Kingdom taking some time to gather all the facts and figures and although we were not awarded the contract, it was a valuable lesson for me, learning about further business tactics in London. Also, I met a variety of people including the daughter of a transporter in, I think, Huddersfield, a very large, jolly lass in her twenties who was thoroughly reliable and hardly experienced any labour problems. This fact was obvious when she arrived in the office one day and greeted my slightly built friend with a rousing "Hi" and a thump on the back, that sent him pirouetting across the tasting room.

However, the pressure continued and at the back of my mind there was always the nudge that my two predecessors had died in harness – and my successor was to do likewise. I had a long hard think when I was approached by one of the three, first hand tea Brokers, and after due consideration became a tea broker myself.

Their office was in Middlesex Street and we used to pick our way through the rubbish that had blown along from Petticoat Lane on a Monday morning. Little did I know, but a few years later our son Malcolm would work for this company, not as a taster, but an accountant. At present, though I had my introduction to tea broking including selling as an auctioneer from the box in the London Auction, probably one of the very few people who had ever bought and sold tea in the same room. As a buyer, I had bought whilst with Harrisons and Crosfield when there was a boom in prices, caused by supply and demand and a packer in Montreal had asked us to obtain supplies in London. I secured some teas at over £3.00 per pound, then a record price in London and the boom encouraged Garland of the Daily Telegraph to produce a cartoon entitled 'Storm in a tea cup' featuring a minister, Roy Hattersley, being tossed around in a large cup of tea. Keen to obtain the original, I telephoned the newspaper and was connected straight through to the man himself. I was promised the cartoon free of charge, provided the Minister did not request it within ten days and later received a telephone call from the Daily Telegraph to advise that the original cartoon was ready for my collection so I handed over an envelope with a note of thanks, and the cartoon, framed, is on my study wall.

My introduction to broking had gone well but more was about to unfold. The company owned an eleven percent shareholding in Tea Brokers Central Africa, Limbe, Malawi, whilst a larger London tea broker, fifty one percent and to this shareholder's office I was bidden one day, to be offered the position of Managing Director in Africa. I mentioned that I had never visited Malawi, but part of the offer was to fly me out for ten days to assess the situation – 'provided I did not swan off to Lake Malawi' – without any obligation. I consulted the family, who were as surprised as I was, received their blessing and flew out for a recce.

Firstly, the company was running at a loss and secondly, the Chairman had been described by one international buyer as the most laid back businessman that he had ever met. On arrival, he advised me that my timing on a Thursday was excellent as we were off to Lake Malawi the following day for a long weekend … when in Rome. His office was stacked with airmail editions of the Daily Telegraph, a fridge stocked with cool drinks and beer and a bottle of Gin kept in the cupboard that when poured really generously, he would then slap his right hand with his left exclaiming, "naughty naughty."

Within the remaining days, after what I can only describe as a wonderful long weekend at the Lake, I visited all the buyers, the local auction, the principal tea producers and a few of the tea estates and came to the conclusion that I could turn TBCA around. A good proportion of the work was almost identical to my exposure to tea estate work in South India and Ceylon, I liked all the people I met in the office and throughout the Industry, so after my return and further discussions with the family, I took the plunge and was Malawi bound. Cicely could not join me immediately as Seamus had a year to complete at a day school in Chelmsford, before moving to his boarding school, so she continued as a travel agent in Brentwood but did come out for a visit, that included a weekend at the company cottage on the shores of Lake Malawi.

HATFIELD PEVEREL
FUN FIVE RUN

This is to Certify that

Paul Gunton

took part in the

Five Mile Fun Run

on Saturday, 14th September 1985

and completed the Course

in ___ hour and _39_ minutes. 37s

PHArfield

Chairman,
Village Fayre Committee

HATFIELD PEVEREL FUN RUN CERTIFICATE

ABOARD 'ISKARA' WITH FRANK AND WENDY MULVILLE 1986

YACHTING MONTHLY   80ᵀᴴ BIRTHDAY PARTY
RIVER ORWELL 2ᴺᴰ AUGUST 1986

ALAN LEADS TAR BABY (1939) AND FIREFLY IN THE SAIL PAST.
LEFT TO RIGHT BEHIND,FALCON (1986),ISRRA (1930),TRILLIAN (1972) AND GAY
GALLIARD (1952)

HATFIELD PEVEREL COMMUNITY ASSOCIATION

MEMORIAL HALL STONE   HATFIELD PEVEREL

LAID IN THE WALL OF THE OLD VILLAGE HALL IN THE STREET,BUILT AFTER
THE FIRST WORLD WAR TO COMMEMORATE THE MEN OF THE VILLAGE
WHO DID NOT RETURN. IT WAS FUNDED BY RELATIVES AND LOCAL
BENEFACTORS AND WHEN THE SITE WAS SOLD FOR DEVELOPMENT THE
COMMITTEE OF THE COMMUNITY ASSOCIATION ENSURED THAT THE STONE
WAS SAVED AND INCORPORATED IN THE WALL OF THE NEW BUILDING IN
1982.

HATFIELD PEVEREL
COMMUNITY ASSOCIATION
CHAIRMAN

CAROLINE BOWEN-DAVIES	1975
ANNE HOWARD	1980
JOHN SCOTT	1983
PAUL GUNTON	1986
JENNY MARTIN	1987
VALERIE MOULDING	1989
PETER STRACHAN	1992
BARBARA BROWN	1993
DENIS ASHBY	1994
KEVIN HAGGERTY	1996
JIM COOKE	1999
BOB HILL	2001
JOHN McKERR	2004

HATFIELD PEVEREL COMMUNITY ASSOCIATION

CHAIRMAN

Storm in a teacup.

THE DAILY TELEGRAPH
WEDNESDAY 9TH MARCH 1977

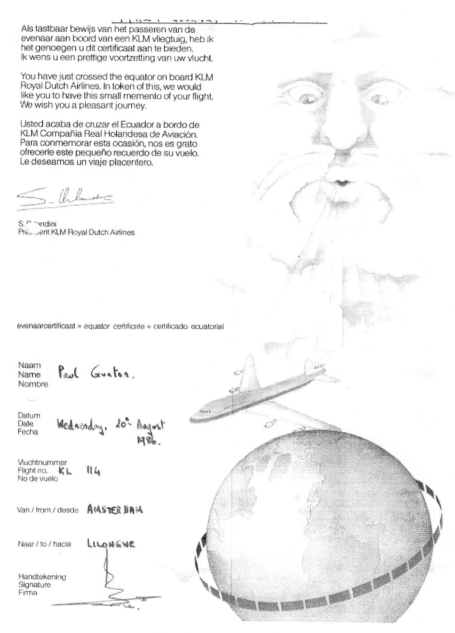

Als tastbaar bewijs van het passeren van de
evenaar aan boord van een KLM vliegtuig, heb ik
het genoegen u dit certificaat aan te bieden.
Ik wens u een prettige voortzetting van uw vlucht.

You have just crossed the equator on board KLM
Royal Dutch Airlines. In token of this, we would
like you to have this small memento of your flight.
We wish you a pleasant journey.

Usted acaba de cruzar el Ecuador a bordo de
KLM Compañia Real Holandesa de Aviación.
Para conmemorar esta ocasión, nos es grato
ofrecerle este pequeño recuerdo de su vuelo.
Le deseamos un viaje placentero.

S. Orlandini
President KLM Royal Dutch Airlines

evenaarcertificaat ∗ equator certificate ∗ certificado ecuatorial

Naam Name Nombre	Paul Gunton.
Datum Date Fecha	Wednesday, 20ᵗʰ August 1986.
Vluchtnummer Flight no. No de vuelo	KL 114
Van / from / desde	AMSTERDAM
Naar / to / hacia	LILONGWE
Handtekening Signature Firma	

FIRST JOURNEY TO MALAWI

70

TEA BROKERS CENTRAL AFRICA LTD.

P.O. BOX 5543, LIMBE, MALAWI

Telephone BLANTYRE: 640 344

Telex: 44149 TEABROCA MI
Fax: 640 462

Directors:

D.A.H. Boddard (Chairman)
P.Gestos (Managing Director)
G.W. Barnes
R. Wrixon
S.B. Zidana

In Association With
Wilson, Smith&& Co. London
Africa Tea Brokers Ltd. Nairobi

This definition on the subject of Brokers was written some time in the last century:-
"It is generally assumed that the first quality a Broker has is a keen intellect, and a lack of cleverness is the defect most frequently attributed to them. But the undoubted value of intelligence should not make us forget other attributes such as his patience, dignity, discretion and reserve, all of which go to make up a Broker's armoury.

A man who relies on his own intellectual superiority is likely to make mistakes that commonsense might have taught him to avoid. The worst defect a Broker can have: excess of zeal, often comes from an exuberant intelligence."

In all modesty we believe that the vintage is continuously improving.

THE WARM HEART OF AFRICA

Before the establishment of Tea Brokers Central Africa by the Chairman some years before, there had been no auction through which the tea producers could offer their teas, so production was either sold privately, or consigned to the London tea auctions. A second broking house had been established and whilst the TBCA total of each auction was averaging sixty three percent more confidence was needed in the system to encourage the producers to entrust larger quantities. Over twelve years, TBCA strove to demonstrate their ability, the auction centre grew, our percentage of the auction at one stage reached 82 percent, the largest auction ever closed at over 23,000 packages, offerings from Mozambique, Zambia and Zimbabwe were obtained and sold successfully and Malawi coffee also appeared in the TBCA catalogue. However, there was a great deal to do initially – and as one fellow director said, 'bite the bullet.'

Initially this was easier said than done, for the Chairman had a contract, through the London shareholders, for another two years, so all executive outgoings were doubled – a second house – two cars – two salaries – airfares. However, after the first financial year, we were in the black but unable to accommodate a dividend, but the day came when the Chairman retired and I was really able to place my feet under the table.

The office was situated on a main road into Limbe, opposite a busy bus stop, two bungalows converted into one long building and containing the tea auction room. This venue changed though to the Tea Association building in Blantyre when quantities increased and of course more time was spent in the room by brokers, buyers and producers. A colourful garden surrounded the building and flowers, entered at the local flower shows, often won awards including a first for St Joseph's lilies One year these flowers did look beautiful in the early morning sunshine so they became one of the company entries but I had no idea of their name until after the prize giving. The office also became a welcome watering hole for the tea planters after tedious drives into town and a welcome haven for their wives to feed and change children. I even baby sat on occasions but was stumped once when a wife rushed in and burst into tears after an altercation with the Limbe Club Manager.

I saw many sights from my window, the curtains had to be drawn by law when the Archbishop of Canterbury passed, (security?); a 40ft container lorry caught alight but the staff were on the scene with the garden hose long before the Blantyre fire brigade arrived when they spent their first two minutes at the scene changing into their uniforms; dancing by large crowds celebrating the election defeat of President Banda followed five years later by riots, protesting against Government policy. The most serious riot became quite dangerous, the crowd from town meeting the Police and Army outside the building - so I evacuated all staff to the back premises and sat tight. After ten minutes I sidled out to check on their welfare and came face to face with a fully armed soldier, R4 submachine gun, additional magazines and tear gas canisters. I enquired why he had entered the building … "ah bwana, I need the toilet." I gave him directions and received a very smart salute on his returning to the fray.

It was important to respect the laws of the land under the rule of President Banda or risk becoming a Prohibited Immigrant – expulsion within twenty four hours. Men were not allowed to grow their hair long and women were banned from wearing long trousers or shorts – except whilst playing golf, or at a Lake shore resort. Prior to leave one year,

TEA BROKERS CENTRAL AFRICA LTD

THE BUNGALOW AT BVUMBWE

THE OFFICE AT LIMBE

QUALITY CONTROL TASTING EVERY FRIDAY

CONDUCTING A WEEKLY TEA AUCTION

Cicely ordered a trouser suit from a Limbe tailor and when I called to collect it, the trousers had not been stitched for fear of making a pair for a lady. I suggested that the trousers could be for myself – "ah, Bwana men do not wear trousers like that in Malawi," so the job was completed by Cicely at home. However, one had to be careful of small talk, several club bar staff were party members and I always thought carefully, before writing the weekly tea market letter for customers overseas.

The international courier service, DHL, spent time one year recording our activities for inclusion in a world promotion film – we used their services every week for tea and coffee sample dispatch to London – and other crops began to interest us also with sales of pepper, cardamom, rhodesgrass seed, citronella oil, and chillies. One weather beaten expatriate chilli producer, from the hills bordering Mozambique, instead of providing us with a sample initially, brought his total annual crop to the office in polysacks that had to be stacked in the garden shed – the smell could have wrecked hundreds of tea samples if they had been stored under the same roof.

The staff had a habit of shopping on a Friday before their often long journey home – their shopping included live chickens who once escaped from their baskets and flew head height through the office towards the front door that was slammed just in time. Fortunately, the long rambling philodendra plant in the foyer was not damaged - it became so long that we sent details and photographs for entry into the Guinness Book of Records but a similar plant growing in South America was some two feet longer and gained the entry for the species.

The office cars took great punishment, indeed, Malawi was judged one of the most dangerous countries worldwide to drive in and it was merciful that we did not have more than one bad accident. A packed express bus trying to overtake us early one morning on the wet, muddy main road, hit the boat trailer, that jack-knifed the car and pushed us sideways along the road before both vehicles nose dived into the ditch. The bus driver disappeared in to the bush, our scarlet Ford Sierra, BG27, was a write off but that was a relief really for with such a distinctive vehicle - everyone knew my movements - and thereafter, we drove

Peugeots. I purchased, though a 1973 VW Beetle for Cicely and at one stage, unable to purchase four identical tyres, we fitted crossplys on the front and radials on the back that made for exciting driving!

Many people wondered why we did not employ a driver and initially Tea Brokers Central Africa did employ one but I soon realised that when I drove I arrived at my destinations considerably more relaxed and thus lowering Cicely's stress levels. The day came therefore when the driver was 'retired' and one vehicle sold. Prior to this event however, one day I was returning to the office via some back roads adjacent to a tea warehouse complex. Parked under a shady tree was the office tea sample van with the driver peacefully dozing, I coasted up to the vehicle and sounded the horn. The effect was instant, physically and mentally – immediate return to consciousness and with an immediate explanation ...... "Ah, Bwana I thought that I was getting a puncture, so I had to park in a quiet place to listen for any air escaping from one of the tyres."

Initially, we flew via Schipol into Stansted on annual leave and experienced two memorable journeys. Once trying to land during the night at Khartoum, we circled the airport for forty minutes in a fierce sandstorm, with full landing lights on that illuminated the billows of sand sweeping across the wings, until the pilot diverted to Cairo. On the second occasion when my steel trunk and baggage had not been unloaded I was grilled thoroughly by a female customs officer at Stansted. However the next day my luggage was delivered to the house in two airline bags together with a small piece of the trunk, marked 'checked baggage.' "Dodgy business" remarked the taxi driver. I telephoned the airline offices at Heathrow and was advised that I had been under surveillance throughout the whole journey and the trunk had been stripped for drugs. I had spent transit time in Lilongwe and Schipol and had packed four kilos of roasted coffee, that apparently defeats even the most competent sniffer dog. Apologies were offered and accepted, also the use of the first class lounge thereafter at Schipol, but five years later I was searched in transit at Schipol: possibly my name had not

78

been erased from the computer. Latterly we flew via Johannesburg into Heathrow.

It was a joy, though, to move into the Company bungalow eight miles out of town, set in a two acre garden that Cicely was to transform. Initially we had lived in a bungalow in Blantyre another in Limbe and also a two story house in Limbe that 'shivered' during the earth tremors one year after the earthquake at Salima. Here, too, we watched a flock of bee eaters feasting on a swarm from the safety of our first floor bedroom, with our dog Robbie who had arrived as a puppy and who was to give us ten years of faithful companionship until bitten by a snake, within the week of Cicely's final departure. His oil painting hangs in my study today....

There was one problem though, a beer hut less than a hundred yards away, that opened for business at dawn every Friday morning – announced by a burst of fire crackers with accompanying very loud music that played all Friday, Saturday and Sunday. Eventually, after negotiations with the village chief, headman, M.P. and Malawi youth pioneer representative, over a crate of beer, it was agreed that I would finance the relocation of the establishment – peace, at last, came to the district. We installed a generator, a new submersible pump in the well, (originally fitted upside down) but we were less successful with the telephone that was out of order for two years until it suddenly rang and Robbie leapt up and barked; astonishingly the call was from a tea contact in Rwanda.

Security became an ever increasing concern and we replaced the two old watchmen with the services of Securicor, had burglar bars fitted to all the windows, a lockable grill across the sitting room /dining room archway, a light on each roof corner of the building, a siren under the roof and in addition we locked every internal door before retiring to bed. This did not stop a pile of leaves being lit one night outside my bathroom window that alerted my acute tea tasting senses and I woke up promptly. I was advised that had this not occurred, I would have been out for the count for several hours waking to a gutted home.

We were only too aware that our next door neighbour had been shot at outside his gate, some planter friends were held up in their lounge whilst another showed me the furrows in his dining room table created by live ammunition. We did not have a gun on the premises, unlike several friends, but I did have a bow and six barbed arrows under the bed at the ready and a fog horn purchased in Guernsey. However, for peace of mind, it was good to have the two Securicor guards on parade each night and they took their duties seriously. I was being collected for dinner one evening and my host enquired on arrival if I was ready, to be advised that I was "preparing myself" – "what on his own?" my host asked. Robbie was sometimes inclined to rise with the sun. I let him out once, realized I had another half hour in hand, and went back to bed, to be aroused by a sharp knocking on the window and a voice advising that Robbie was ready to re-enter the house. The watchman received a short reply. Robbie stayed outside and I never went back to sleep. However, one night the guards locked a local dog in the hen house that killed all the birds, bar one, but they did help me another night in the darkness to remove a local dog from a water tank to save it from drowning. Ever conscious of rabies, I lowered a coffee sack over the edge, so that the dog could claw its way up the hessian surface successfully without any of us handling the animal.

Petty thieving was also a problem … Vegetables … Jams, despite the fact that we provided rations for the staff but once, when items were fast disappearing, I was advised to enlist the help of a witch doctor. He actually looked like a doctor, with a 'practice' in the Limbe Market, complete with white coat, and he did the deed, somehow, as nothing disappeared for a good six months.

Often our neighbours, who lived in thatched mud brick houses, came to the gate requesting flowers for family funerals and TBCA provided a coffin for a garden boy's infant son that I delivered to his village in the bush. As I waited in the car for two members of staff to return from the hut, I listened to the village folk singing whilst an almost full moon rose from behind the range of hills – a moving and magical experience.

Our shopping was mostly achieved from two well stocked supermarkets, the local market, where I presented our butcher with three Irish Meat Board diagrams of how to joint beef, lamb and pork but the cuts did not improve, although the diagrams were always proudly displayed, whilst the Carlsberg brewery produced excellent lager. We also had a huge avocado pear tree in the garden and I took regular buckets for the staff in town and Robbie put on weight in the season and produced a beautiful silky coat.

The lake cottage provided a wonderful weekend retreat, with the verandah steps leading straight into the water. However, it had been neglected and we had it rewired, a bedroom was demolished, as I could place my arm through a crack on the "seaward" side, and many wire baskets full of rock were lowered in front, to halt erosion. Bats came out of the roof like starlings at dusk and hippos were constant neighbours, Malcolm lying up one evening on his windsurfer offshore, until one moved away and one chomped the mooring buoy for good measure. The plot itself was otherwise a spacious garden, with palm trees and a sandy beach, used one moonlit night by a herd of hippo, when a calf was born outside our bedroom window and on another, when a group of fishermen repaired their nets, singing Christmas carols in their own language. Robbie, too, loved his visits, sitting in the water up to his neck after his long hot drives but he did earn his keep catching rats, one under our double bed early in the morning. Sailing was a pleasure and our *Enterprise* was a dinghy to really enjoy but again, hippo had to be watched and I had eight around me once, becalmed for an hour, a mile offshore. It was a case of mutual admiration. I gazed at them and they grumped, blew and gazed back at me.

At Christmas one year, the water level at the bottom of the steps was lapping my ankles but by Easter, at the same spot, the level was above my head. The additional weight on the earth's surface must have been colossal, the Lake being an area 365 miles long and 52 miles wide with miles of beautiful coastline from numerous golden beaches, stunning cliffs, uninhabited islands, shoals of multi coloured fish, some unique to the lake, to several historic sites dating from the early missionary days. The earthquake a few weeks later came almost at midnight like a 747 flying low over the water, the garden buckled under my feet, the pipe against the tank was banging away, coconuts cascaded from the trees, birds woke up – but there was not even a ripple on the water – apparently, due to the epicentre being very deep in the earth's surface – but three people were killed due to structural damage and after-shocks occurred for several weeks.

The time came when it was decided to sell the cottage for it was underutilized and always required attention. We arrived for one weekend to find the power line almost at ground level, so I ferreted out the electricity supply company in nearby Mangochi but it was difficult to explain the problem, so I took pencil to paper and immediately solved the language barrier – "Ah bwana, you have droop." The decision to sell was fortuitous for within a year the Lake level dropped many feet, a beach developed in front of the property and security problems escalated.

Our other recreational areas were the beautiful Zomba Plateau and further away, dominating some tea estates, Mulanje Mountain, a spectacular massif with several peaks and on the plateau, several well equipped mountain huts, managed by the mountain club. We made many weekend treks for a night or two and occasionally scaled any nearby peak from a hut and in my last year, when Cicely had returned to Ireland, I spent seven weekends on the Mountain and climbed Sapetwa, the roof of Malawi, at 9,855 feet. The other extreme of temperature was the heat of the Lower Shire valley all of 200 ft, where a large part of the sugar industry is situated, together with the well established Sucoma club. I once called at the nearby convent and was invited in to the refectory for refreshment, where the Nun opened her 'fridge and I was astonished and impressed to find that it was full of Carlsberg beer. "Ah" said the nun, "I have been in Malawi, much longer than yourself."

Visits to tea estates were frequent and necessary, to keep abreast of the planting conditions and every Friday morning I visited three tea factories including a decaffeinated plant for tasting and quality control purposes. The main districts were in easy striking distance and TBCA sponsored golf tournaments in both the district clubs, one memorable year being when Cicely won the annual Ladies Plate and Seamus the Gentlemen's Mug, in Mulanje.

Eight hours drive northwards from the office there were two tea estates and one factory opened for production in 1987 when I was asked to visit and assess the initial teas. I spent the first four days on the factory floor with the non English speaking gang, opening every tea sack, sorting grades, drawing individual samples, weighing each sack, producing weight notes, itemizing invoices, producing invoice samples and after tasting and valuing the individual samples, they were distributed to all tea buyers in Limbe who purchased the 2,199.6 kilos within two days. The estate prospered under very efficient management and it was not long before TBCA was selling over one million kilos of the production, annually.

It was an interesting part of the world, for at the southernmost area of the estate, slaves had been rested, after trekking for miles, before being led over the adjacent hill to the beach at Chintetchi and onward across the Lake and beyond. As they rested they dropped seeds from their regions – often far away from Malawi – that have since grown into mature vegetation. There is a huge macadamia acreage, too, once the largest single macadamia estate in the world, the nuts being processed in a facility next to the tea factory and creating a significant macadamia honey business. Coffee once thrived but this crop was uprooted as coffee berry disease spread south from Kenya and through Tanzania. I trekked up to the head waters of the water supply in the hills, through the bush one afternoon with the manager, and at one stage we met two people hunting who said that they had only seen two white men before and that was twenty-four moons ago – the surveyors for the pipeline.

The Mombasa auctions had attracted, successfully, teas from neighbouring foreign countries, so to establish Limbe as a wider international tea auction centre, we succeeded in offering teas from Mozambique, Zimbabwe and Zambia, the latter territory being handled by my able Malawian director. Mozambique had been ravaged by years of civil war, with many tea factories being shelled or burnt out, with tea bushes untended, growing up to fifteen feet high. My first visit was to

Milange district, bordering Malawi, then Garue district the first journey taking nearly seven hours for a journey of less than 200km through deserted, shattered, villages, scarcely any animal or bird in sight over untended roads and over river beds where bridges had been destroyed. Two years later, the same journey took less than three hours, the people had regained their pride and happiness and Garue town had blossomed from near desertion to a thriving community with street café's, umbrella shaded tables on the pavements, offering chilled cans of South African beer, and my Portuguese host even taking me to the friendly colourful Domino night club.

Zimbabwe tea estates are set amidst beautiful countryside and we sold production from four factories visiting our clients certainly every other year and rather than fly, we travelled by air conditioned Stagecoach transport from Malawi and through Mozambique, collecting a vehicle in Harare. On my first visit unwittingly, I picked up a hitch hiker, something that I was recommended never to repeat, but we talked for over an hour before his set down point where he offered me a Zimbabwe dollar to buy a drink on my way back to the Capital, but I declined his generosity. It was on this journey that I was invited to pull in to a ranch for tea; the ranch was surrounded by a high, stout, wire fence, the gates displaying the sobering notice 'Beware Lion'. I drove along the avenue to the homestead, opened the door and hesitated – two lionesses were sauntering over to welcome the new guest, cheerful greetings were shouted from the verandah and the three of us padded over the lawn together.

I also visited the southern tea estates in Tanzania but really, it was more logical for the producers to utilize the Mombasa auctions for this centre was significantly closer to their estates and their produce could be delivered, stored and offered from warehouses close to the deep water port.

I could have negotiated a further contract but Cicely reminded me wisely that two years older, retirement would not be any easier, so we made plans to settle in Ireland, she packed up the house, supervised the loading of the 20 ft container and left on the 17 March 1998 via Brazil to stay with Seamus on his first overseas contract. Sadly two days earlier Robbie had died from a snake bite but for the faithful dog of ten years, he would probably have found it difficult to adjust to a new home and accept a new master's voice. I sold the *Enterprise* to an old friend, the Ndirande Sailing Club Blantyre had granted me life membership and I had re-established sailing on the City's Mudi dam, after an absence of twenty years. Also, I had become the organic signatory for Malawi certifying the production of organic produce prior to export - a host of memories I reflected upon during my final weeks with the knowledge that my last trading year produced a record turnover, 17 million kilos, the most healthy bottom line and the highest dividend for Tea Brokers Central Africa Limited.

As the South African Airways flight climbed away from the Republic of Malawi, I was thankful that I had made that decision to become a Tea Broker, fourteen years earlier.

ON THE ROOF OF MALAWI. SAPITWA PEAK 9,855 FEET

MULANJE MASSIF 1105 HRS SUNDAY 14 JUNE 1998

NAMASELI PEAK MALAWI MOZAMBIQUE BORDER
CLIMBED FROM NGAPANI ESTATE MANGOCHI

NOT DEAD YET

Happily, I enjoyed two tea consultancies after Cicely and I moved our home from Essex to the west of Ireland.

The first was to Mauritius when the family who own the oldest tea estate on the island invited me to spend a month on site, to work in the factory and also the field, with a particular brief to improve the standard of green leaf being plucked for delivery to their factory, as the majority of the leaf for manufacture is grown by smallholders. 'Good tea is made in the field' was the maxim in India, so declining the offer of a car and driver, I used to set forth at 0700 hrs in the collection lorries. The initial response to my appearance at the weighing points was surprise and shyness but, shortly, I was being invited to family plots where I gained information on yields and management, including fertilizer applications. Their total production is packaged and sold in Mauritius and we remain in close contact with my assistance still being sought from time to time.

My second secondment took me for two months to Southern Tanzania, to an estate that I had visited a few years before but which was now under new management. My brief there was to observe leaf and factory conditions, recommend improvements as soon as they presented themselves and taste manufacture daily for quality control purposes. The location was a long day's drive from Dar-es-salaam in the southern highlands, at an altitude of over 6,000 ft and one morning, just after dawn, I was in a tea field surrounded by pluckers who were singing as the sun climbed against an almost cloudless sky. A magical scene but a few thousand miles away the second Iraq war was in its third week – life is continually brittle.

However, as I began my journey home, I decided that Tanzania should be my tea swansong. Time goes on, with so many changes in the business world and I have seen several consultants striving to keep up with the times and sometimes not succeeding too well. On that journey, we stopped at a large junction where there was a high pole with an umbrella thatch, under which there were numerous Africans who beckoned me enthusiastically to join them. BBC world news was being screened direct from Iraq in to the African bush. Bite the bullet, I thought, the time has come to be thankful for forty five years in the tea trade.

In an era, too, that had seen the demise of the London tea auctions, accelerated in a small way by the growth of the Limbe tea auction centre through which more and more tea produced in Malawi was being sold and not shipped for sale in the London terminal auction. The Tea Trade, in fact, is now a shadow of its former self with many companies no longer in existence, including my first, second and third employers and the largest London shareholder of Tea Brokers Central Africa.

Happily, though, we continue to have close links with many friends worldwide and recently, the owner of one of the family owned Malawi tea estate companies and his wife stayed with us in Ireland and I attended a tea trade gathering on the *Cutty Sark*. All through the years there has never been a person who I would not like to meet again and in my Brokering years, I always, looked on teas entrusted to Tea Brokers Central Africa to sell, as my own property, until they were sold at a price fully justified to producer and buyer.

I have never forgotten the farewell advice of the old commissionaire as I left the city office in 1959 en route to Cochin for the first time, "Paul, good luck, don't discuss politics, religion and sex overseas, and you will be all right."

QUALITY CONTROL TEA TASTING

KIBENA TEA FACTORY TANZANIA

However, two years ago Cicely gave me a book entitled "Not Dead Yet" and I thought that this was a pretty good positive approach to life at my age.

In 1995, a family friend of over forty years standing founded an orphanage in India at Chinnammalpuram village in Tamil Nadu State, forty six miles from the tip of the sub continent, Kanyakumari, where the Arabian Sea, the Bay of Bengal and the Indian Ocean meet. The area is very rural, under populated and well off the tourist trail. After a nudge or two I spent nine weeks in 2005 at Kings Children's Village with sixty six of the children and although I had never taught before, and arrived on site inexperienced and with a stiff upper lip honed by forty five years in the commercial world, the children had melted that lip within a week and in many ways taught me to teach them. Their age group was five to twelve years, girls and boys and my teaching responsibilities also included hours at the village school, a hundred yards along the dusty street.

Since then moved by this experience, I have written letters to relatives, friends and tea trade contacts who have responded from numerous parts of the world, donating to date, £18,295.20p a magnificent effort. This book was written during my second visit in 2006, teaching where I left off amidst a background of happy chatter. I felt that I had to return after two little boys telephoned me at home in Ireland and said, "Uncle, when are you coming?" Since then I have paid a third visit in January 2008. I realise only too well that my contribution to life here is but a drop in the ocean but every drop creates a ripple that in this case, has lapped into so many young lives. There has been a backwash, too, for I now look on the world with much more compassion and I am just thankful that I have had the opportunity to contribute a little to life that has been for me, so rewarding.

Also, so much mutual trust and affection has been established and I have often recalled the words of a Japanese gentleman who said to me at Karachi Airport years ago …

"Remember, a smile is an international passport."

90

There are sixty seven passport holders here, sixty six ever smiling youngsters and their teacher and companion, Paul Uncle.

Kings Children's Village
Chinnammalpuram
Tamil Nadu
South India

February 2006

KINGS WORLD TRUST FOR CHILDREN (INDIA)

940 Chinnammalpuram, Dhalapathi Samudram (P.O)
Tirunelveli Dt., S.India - 627 101.
Tel : 04637 287167 Fax : 04637 287367
E-mail : kingsworld@sancharnet.in

This book was born out of my first visit to the Kings World Trust for Children in 2005. My subsequent visits have only increased my desire to publicise the marvellous work being carried out here.

SELVA PRIYA - UMA - MELBA - ATHI

SANDAL - JOHN JACOB - ALWYN - PAUL- UNCLE MOSES - SAM - SANDY

THE HAPPY FAMILY 4 MARCH 2006

Volunteer Teachers wanted in India

- Taking a career break
- Planning a working Holiday
- Want a New Start
- Just Getting Away from it all

Then why not come to India and teach disadvantaged children at Kings English School
- All subject teachers welcome
- One to six month placements.

Come with or without family

KINGS WORLD TRUST FOR CHILDREN

Volunteers . The Trust is managed and administered in the UK entirely by volunteers. The Trust also operates a 'Volunteer' programme in India. The Trust welcomes applications from volunteers who are medically qualified, TEFL and craft teachers and young people with commitment or special skills. Volunteers pay their own travel costs and for their food and living expenses while staying at the Trust's visitor accommodation. Around 30 volunteers are accepted each year.

Trust Policy . The Trust operates an equal opportunities policy both in the UK and in India. Children, Staff and Volunteers are selected regardless of race, sex, colour, faith, caste, background or physical handicap.

Funding. Funds to support the work of the Trust are raised by the following methods :
'Child Sponsorship Scheme', Gift Aid donations, Individual and Corporate donations, 'Grant Making Trusts', Companies, Schools, Churches, Clubs, Wills & Bequests, Stockport Charity Shop, Special Fund Raising Events.

For further information on supporting the work of the Trust or on opportunities for volunteers please contact :

Kings World Trust for Children
7 Deeptene
Haslemere, Surrey, GU27 1RE
United Kingdom
Tel & Fax : 01428 653804   E-mail : kwtc@basicmere.com   Charity number : 1024972

Kings World Trust for Children (India)
940 Chinnammapuram,
Dhalapathi Samadram P.O
Thenkhali District - 627 101
Tamil Nadu, South India.
Tel : 04637 287167. Fax : 04637 287367 E-mail : kingsworld@sancharnet.in
Website : www.kingschildren.org

KINGS WORLD TRUST FOR CHILDREN

"The Trust is not an institution, it is a real home for children who have never known love, care and security in their lives. They become part of a unique family committed to giving them a childhood and a sustainable future through education and training"

The Kings World Trust for Children was founded in 1995 to provide a caring home, a formal education and skills training for orphan, homeless and poor children in South India.

KINGS ENGLISH SCHOOL

Kindergarten

Kindergarten Children

School Office

Junior School

KINGS WORLD TRUST FOR CHILDREN

VOLUNTEER CERTIFICATE

This is to certify that ....MR. PAUL GUNTON...
was a volunteer in India with Kings World Trust for Children

From ....12.01.05 to 17.03.05....08.01.06 to 17.03.06....&...19.01.08.to.19.03.08...

The Trust provides a caring home, an education & skills training for orphan and homeless children & young people in South India.

His / Her contribution to the work of the Trust was very much appreciated.

Date : 18/3/08

Trustee / Director

7 Deepdene Haslemere Surrey GU27 1RE, UK Tel & Fax : 01428-653504, E-mail : kwtc@haslemere.com

940 Chinnammalpuram, Dhalapathisamudram (P.O.), Tirunelveli Dist., South India
Tel : 04637-329988 & 329696   Fax : 04637-287367 E-mail : trust@kingsindia.in

96

KINGS WORLD TRUST FOR CHILDREN (INDIA)

940 Chinnammalpuram, Dhalapathi Samudram (P.O)
Tirunelveli Dt., S.India - 627 101.
Tel : 04637 - 329988 & 329696 Fax : 04637 287367
E-mail : trust@kingsindia.in

Leap Year Day 2008

Dear

I received such a rapturous welcome when I returned to the orphanage last month, both from the staff, and, particularly, the children and despite an absence of two years, we all slotted back happily together again within a day. I have resumed teaching at two of the Government schools that the children attend, assisting with evening homework, outdoor activities, and at weekends, the coastal picnics or trips into the adjacent, beautiful, Western Ghat mountains are days filled with happiness. There is never a dull moment and my days are certainly much longer than those I spend in Ireland – and yet I have no desire to have a siesta and certainly feel younger in this vibrant community.

However, realistically, I think that this, my third visit, will be my last, for Cicely finds my absences away from home not easy and I have had two health nudges recently, reminding me that I am not as young as I used to be – I am seventy years old in October, (I can't believe it!) – so I am presently enjoying the swansong. In this regard, I have decided to send a copy of this letter as a 'one off' to everyone who was sent a copy of my letter dated 15th March 2005 and 1st March 2006 and with apologies to some people who have already requested that their names be deleted from the address list for Trust newsletters and correspondence every six months. Their earlier requests have been respected already and that address list is amended. However, if there are also others who no longer wish to receive further correspondence, please just advise the Haslemere office, to save the Trust printing and postal costs, but the website www.kingschildren.org can always be viewed for the very latest information.

As you may recall, the Founder of the Trust, Colin Wagstaff, is a very old family friend and knew Cicely from visits to Ireland before she and I married in 1967, and in England, he manages the Trust from his home in Haslemere. Overheads there are minimal with at least 95% of funding being directed straight to India where it is administered directly by Colin and a very competent Indian Director.

When the Paul Uncle Fund was established in 2005, I thought that response would be in the region of £1000.00-there is no financial backing from any international organization - so I am overwhelmed by the response that still continues to increase with a monthly bankers order in place, and, as at the 1st February 2008, totals: Sterling £16567.30p Indian Rupees 1,317,345.00.

The generous euro donations I have converted to sterling figures, on the day of receipt at the current rate of exchange to obtain a direct sterling / rupee comparison and certainly the end figure is a very significant total locally that has made a marked contribution to the Trust funds. Response has been received from numerous individuals throughout the World, sponsorship from a team in the Newcastle – upon – Tyne half marathon, several companies and the Irish Association of St. Lazarus. To all you who have contributed, my heartfelt thanks.

Attached herewith are some slips to accompany further donations that I do hope you will consider whenever possible – the cause is so worthy, and, as before, I have requested not to be advised of individual donations but I will keep in regular contact with the Haslemere office for details of the running total – the Paul Uncle Fund will never close. Also, I will continue to be the Trust Secretary in Ireland and interview all Irish volunteers after their applications have been received.

I will never forget the periods that I have spent here..... these windows in my retirement have been magical and quite unexpected when I left Malawi in 1999. Every day, though, has generated a pang or two, particularly one this year within ten days of my arrival. A little boy – completely unconnected with the Trust but who I taught at the village school three years ago along with the youngest Trust children – heard that I had returned and came to find me. Shyly, he presented me with a little note book that he had made and on the front page he has written:

"My dear Friend Paul Uncle present to
Arul Raj
Never will I leave you: never will I forsake you
Hebrews 13:56 "

A crystal reflection of the mutal Trust and affection that bonds the children and myself in this special haven in Tamil Nadu. I will always treasure this little book and the fondest memories that will never fade.

Happy Days

Paul Uncle / Paul Gunton

Kings World Trust for Children
7 Deepdene
Haslemere, Surrey GU27 1RE
United Kingdom

Charity No. : 1024872
Tel : 01428 653 504
E-mail : kwtc@haslemere.com
Website : www.kingschildren.org
www.kingsenglishschool.com

Paul Uncle Fund

Please find enclosed herewith my donation for _____

Yours faithfully

Kings World Trust for Children
7 Deepdene
Haslemere, Surrey GU27 1RE
United Kingdom

Charity No. : 1024872
Tel : 01428 653 504
E-mail : kwtc@haslemere.com
Website : www.kingschildren.org
www.kingsenglishschool.com

Paul Uncle Fund

Please find enclosed herewith my donation for _____

Yours faithfully

Kings World Trust for Children
7 Deepdene
Haslemere, Surrey GU27 1RE
United Kingdom

Charity No. : 1024872
Tel : 01428 653 504
E-mail : kwtc@haslemere.com
Website : www.kingschildren.org
www.kingsenglishschool.co...

Paul Uncle Fund

Please find enclosed herewith my donation for _____

Yours faithfully

Kings World Trust for Children
7 Deepdene
Haslemere, Surrey GU27 1RE
United Kingdom

Charity No. : 1024872
Tel : 01428 653 504
E-mail : kwtc@haslemere.com
Website : www.kingschildren.org
www.kingsenglishschool.com

Paul Uncle Fund

Please find enclosed herewith my donation for _____

Yours faithfully

KINGS WORLD TRUST FOR CHILDREN (INDIA)

940 Chinnammalpuram, Dhalapathi Samudram (P.O)
Tirunelveli Dt., S.India - 627 101.
Tel : 04637 287167 Fax : 04637 287367
E-mail : kingsworld@sancharnet.in

1ˢᵗ March 2006

Dear,

It was always my intention to return as a volunteer to teach English at this orphanage, in rural Tamil Nadu, after my moving and rewarding nine weeks last year, living with the sixty six children, but not quite so soon, indeed, I felt fulfilled when I returned to Ireland. However, as the weeks passed, I became, mentally, more and more restive and when two little boys telephoned me in August and said, "Uncle when are you coming?" I decided to return at the same time this year for a similar period.

The children and I have just picked up from where we left off last year that has been ideal. Teaching, and at the local village school, has continued happily and weekend picnics, visits to nearby Kanyakumari – the tip of the sub continent – and the nearby hills have been fun. The swimming pool has been completed and although the Enterprise dinghy is now on the coast at the village, adopted by the Trust after the Tsunami, she has not been launched – too much other activity!

The status of the Trust continues unaltered, not backed by any international organisation but stimulated by a loyal, small group of people, who are dedicated, efficient and enthusiastic, with the office in England at our friend's home in Haslemere. Therefore, overhead expenses there are minimal with at least 95% of funding being directed straight to India to be administed by a very competent board of trustees. There has been one change recently, though, for the Trust now has a new Patron, Penelope Keith, who needs no introduction after her wonderful television appearances.

After my visit last year I composed a letter, posted to relatives, friends and Tea Trade contacts who responded from numerous parts of the world, donating, to date, a magnificent sum of £ 6014.04p and still growing, due to a monthly banker's order. The Trust has requested a copy of my address list, to include details on their mailing list for distribution of the newsletter every six months, but we both respect the fact that not everybody would be interested, in which case, please, just advise the Haslemere office – also to save the Trust printing and posting costs. In the meantime, their website www.kingschildren.org can always be viewed for the very latest information.

100

I do not expect people to respond so generously to this letter but I would ask that you do not forget this very special place and consider sending any donations, whenever possible, accompanied by one of the attached slips, or just with an attached note 'For Paul uncle fund,' thereby enabling these funds to be listed separately from others received. Like last year, I have requested not to be advised of individual donations but I will contact the Haslemere office from time to time for the running total.

Meantime, I have gently spread the word amongst the children that I can not visit them every year that they seem to understand – our mutual affection and deep trust are even stronger this year. However, I aim to revisit in four years time when many of the five to twelve year old girls and boys who I have taught, will be teenagers, well on the way to becoming responsible adults who the Republic of India will, I am certain, be justly proud.

I am only too aware, though, that my contribution here is but 'a drop in the ocean' but every drop creates a ripple that in this case has lapped into so many young lives and there has been a backwash, too, for I now look on life with much more compassion. Also, I am just so grateful to have found such rewarding work as a volunteer overseas and I have now become the secretary for the Trust in Ireland, so the link in my absence from here, will continue strongly.

I have never forgotten the words of a Japanese gentleman who I met at Karachi airport years ago ....

'Remember a smile is an international passport'

There are sixty seven passport holders here, sixty six ever smiling youngsters and their teacher and companion, Paul uncle.

(Carrowntawy House, Ballymote, Sligo, Ireland)

101

Kings World Trust for Children
7, Deepdene
Haslemere, Surrey GU27 1RE
United Kingdom

Charity No. : 1024872
Tel   : 01428 653 504
Fax   : 01428 653 504
E-mail : kwtc@haslemere.com

Paul Uncle Fund

Please find enclosed herewith my donation for _____

Yours faithfully

Kings World Trust for Children
7, Deepdene
Haslemere, Surrey GU27 1RE
United Kingdom

Charity No.: 1024872
Tel   : 01428 653 504
Fax   : 0 1428 653 504
E-mail : kwtc@haslemere.com

Paul Uncle Fund

Please find enclosed herewith my donation for _____

Yours faithfully

Kings World Trust for Children
7, Deepdene
Haslemere, Surrey GU27 1RE
United Kingdom

Charity No. : 1024872
Tel   : 01428 653 504
Fax   : 01428 653 504
E-mail : kwtc@haslemere.com

Paul Uncle Fund

Please find enclosed herewith my donation for _____

Yours faithfully

KINGS WORLD TRUST FOR CHILDREN (INDIA)

940 Chinnammalpuram, Dhalapathi Samudram (P.O)
Tirunelveli Dt., S.India - 627 101.
Tel : 04637 287167 Fax : 04637 287367
E-mail : kingsworld@sancharnet.in

Sunset, 15 March 2005

Dear,

The sun has just dipped below the skyline of the Western Ghats, a stunning backdrop to the surrounding countryside, and creating a stark silhouette against a crimson sky in this underpopulated, very rural area of South India, 47 kms from the tip of the Indian subcontinent, Kanyakumari.

Since our return to Ireland in 1999, and following two consultancies on tea estates in Mauritius and Tanzania, I have had a growing desire to assist, in some way, a worthy cause, as a grateful token for the life that I have enjoyed to date – and before I become too old.

It took little more than a nudge from an old family friend, who knew Cicely, my wife, before we first met in 1963, to jump at Colin Wagstaff's suggestion to come here as a volunteer to teach English at the Kings World Trust For Children, an orphanage that he founded in 1995, after a career in the army. Progress has been remarkable and from the enclosed literature and from their website: www.kingschildren.org you will be able to appreciate just what has been achieved in ten years.

However, there was just one hurdle to negotiate – I had never taught, let alone English – but I booked flights in October, bought two TEFL books, studied studiously and arrived here within three weeks of the Tsunami that devastated miles of the nearby coastline. For the past nine weeks, I have lived at Kings School Village, with sixty five of the children, taught five to twelve year old girls and boys on site, and at the local village school, a hundred yards along the dusty street, dominated by the church, accompanied them swimming and on various weekend outings, sometimes into the hills through beautiful countryside. Sailing tuition was also on my brief and I rigged the Enterprise during my first weekend but the coast remains a very sensitive area and out of deep respect, the dinghy has not been launched. Swimming tuition, too, has not been practical, for the builders who were putting the final touches to the new pool, were diverted to the coastal village that the Trust has 'adopted' for reconstruction - as well as providing new fishing nets for the community.

I am only too aware of the generosity of the public, worldwide, to the various Tsunami appeals but undaunted, I am writing to all our relatives and friends on our Christmas card list and to several friends in the Tea Trade who I have known during the forty five years spent in the Trade, twenty eight years of which were in producing countries, in the hope that you may consider sending a donation to the Trust, accompanied by the tear-off slip below.

This Trust, as you can gather, is not backed by any international organizations but stimulated by a loyal, small group of people who are dedicated, efficient and enthusiastic. Overhead expenses in England are minimal, the Trust office is in the study of Colin's home in England, so virtually 95% of funding comes direct to the Trust in India, where every child is known by their Christian name. One big happy family, infact.

For my part, I have had an experience that I will never forget over a period of nine weeks that has established much mutual affection and profound trust . I am returning to Ireland fulfilled but I will certainly miss the calls of 'Paul Uncle' that have echoed constantly around this village, a very special place in South India.

Finally, I have requested not to be advised of any individual donations, just the total amount that has been donated by the time that the account closes on the 30th June 2005, a few weeks before my sixty seventh birthday.

(Carrowntawy House, Ballymote, Sligo. Ireland 00353.71.91.83936)

Fourt

Kings World Trust for Children
7, Deepdene
Haslemere, Surrey GU27 1RE
United Kingdom

Charity No : 1024872
Tel   : +44 (0) 1428 653 504
Fax   : +44 (0) 1428 653 504
E-mail : kwtc@haslemere.com

In response to Paul Guntons letter dated 15 March 2005 please find enclosed herewith my donation for _____

Yours faithfully

The letter that raised £6004. 04p

104

THE FAMILY - AT HOME

II AUGUST 2006

MALCOLM ANNIE SEAMUS

CICELY PAUL

ZANZI AIDAN

APPENDIX

ENTER THE REAL WORLD

HARRISONS & CROSFIELD,
LIMITED.

LONDON, CALCUTTA, COCHIN,
COLOMBO, DJAKARTA, KOZHIKODE, MEDAN,
MONTREAL, QUILON, TORONTO, VANCOUVER.

CABLES & TELEGRAMS:
HARRICROS, LONDON.

TELEPHONE:
MANSION HOUSE 4333.

1 to 4, Great Tower Street,
London, E.C.3.

8th November, 19 57

REPLY TO _____ Branches _____ DEPT.

P. Gunton, Esq.,
c/o Mrs. Hunt,
Stonehouse Cottage,
Gressenhall Road,
London, S.W.18.

Dear Sir,

We are glad to advise you that we have now received
your medical report and references, and that we have
pleasure in confirming your appointment on the terms
stated in our letter of the 4th November.

We look forward to your starting here next Monday,
the 11th November.

Yours faithfully,
HARRISONS & CROSFIELD, LIMITED.

Branches Secretary.

107

HARRISONS & CROSFIELD.
LIMITED.

LONDON, CALCUTTA, COCHIN.
COLOMBO, DJAKARTA, KOZHIKODE, MEDAN,
MONTREAL, QUILON, TORONTO, VANCOUVER.

CABLES & TELEGRAMS:
HARRICROS, LONDON.

TELEPHONE:
MANSION HOUSE 4333.

1 to 4, Great Tower Street,
London, E.C.3.

2nd October, 19 58.

REPLY TO .... Branches .... DEPT.

P. Gunton, Esq.

Dear Sir,

      We write to advise you that, as a result of a
review of the salaries applicable to Eastern Trainees, it
has been decided to pay you a salary at the rate of £450
per annum as from 1st October this year.

      This increased salary at the rate of £450 per
annum takes into account the increase on the former scale
which you would have received on your attaining your 20th
birthday this month.

      Yours faithfully,
    HARRISONS & CROSFIELD, LIMITED,

Branches Secretary.

HARRISONS & CROSFIELD.
LIMITED.

LONDON, CALCUTTA, CALICUT,
COCHIN, COLOMBO, DJAKARTA, MEDAN,
MONTREAL, QUILON, TORONTO, VANCOUVER.

CABLES & TELEGRAMS:
HARRICROS, LONDON.

TELEPHONE:
MANSION HOUSE 4333.

1 to 4, *Great Tower Street,*
London, E.C.3.

15th June, 19 59

REPLY TO Branches DEPT.

P. Gunton Esq.,
Tea Department.

Dear Sir,

We have pleasure in confirming that the terms of
your appointment in South India would be as follows:-

Salary   At the rate of Rs.925 per month, rising at
          the commencement of the second year of the
          agreement to Rs.950 per month and at the
          commencement of the third year to Rs.1,000
          per month, and of the fourth year to Rs.1,025
          per month.

C.O.L.A.   At the rate current from time to time. This
          is paid at the discretion of the Board and
          varies in accordance with a Cost of Living Index
          figure. It is now at the rate of Rs.400
          per month.

This remuneration will commence on the date on which
you take up your duties in Cochin.

Passage and Outfit)
Allowance. Clauses)   As in the Agreement.
4 and 5.   )

Your engagement generally will be subject to the
terms of our letter of 4th November, 1957, and to the
Eastern Staff First Agreement, three copies of which are
enclosed embodying the salary set out above. We should
be glad if you would sign and return to us all three copies
for completion, and one completed copy will be returned to you
for your retention.

contd.

It is understood that you are prepared to remain
unmarried for your first tour of service in the East.

Yours faithfully,
HARRISONS & CROSFIELD, LIMITED.

Branches Secretary.

Encls.

500/10-58

Dated the 15th _day of_ June 1959

Memorandum

of

Agreement
(First)

BETWEEN

HARRISONS & CROSFIELD LIMITED

AND

PAUL GUNTON

Memorandum of Agreement made

this   fifteenth   day of   June   One
thousand nine hundred and   fifty nine   BETWEEN
HARRISONS & CROSFIELD, LIMITED   whose
Registered Office is at 1-4, Great Tower Street, London, E.C.3.
, carrying on business at that
address and elsewhere (hereinafter called " the Company ") of the one
part

AND   PAUL GUNTON
of   Point Cottage, Port Navas, Falmouth
(hereinafter called " the Employee ") of the other part
WHEREBY it is agreed by and between the parties hereto as follows :—

1. THE Company appoints the Employee in the business of the Company *Nature of appointment*
as carried on by them at- in South India.
or elsewhere in the East for a period of four years computed as hereinafter
mentioned, subject nevertheless to the provisions stipulations and conditions
hereinafter contained.

2. THE Company may transfer the Employee from any one Office to any *Transfer of Employee*
other Office of the Company or to any Office belonging to one of the Companies
with which the Company is associated in which latter case the Employee will
enter into a new Agreement with the Associated Company to which he is transferred such new Agreement running for the unexpired portion of this Agreement
and being identical with it in other respects except for any alterations in salary
which may be appropriate in accordance with the provisions of Clause 6 hereof
and thereupon this Agreement shall be terminated and cease to have effect.

3. THE aforesaid period of four years shall be deemed to commence and *Date of commencement of Agreement*
this Agreement shall, save as hereinafter appears, be deemed to operate from the
date when the Employee enters upon his duties hereunder, whereof the certificate
of the Resident Directors or Director or the Manager for the time being of the
Company's business at the Office aforesaid shall be conclusive evidence and final
and binding on the Company and the Employee.

4. (*a*) THE Company will on the signing hereof lend to the Employee a *Passage money*
sufficient sum in cash as will provide him with a passage (by sea or air in accordance
with the Company's regulations in force from time to time) from the point of
embarkation in the United Kingdom to the Office for which he is engaged.

(*b*) THE Company will also lend to the Employee, the sum of £50 sterling *Outfit allowances*
or its equivalent in local currency at the then rate of exchange, for outfit and
expenses incurred by him meantime.

1

(c) IF at the expiration of six calendar months from the date of the Employee entering upon his duties hereunder the Employee shall not then give notice in writing to the Company of his intention to determine this Agreement under Clause 14 hereof and if he shall in the meantime have satisfactorily performed his obligations hereunder, the Company will also lend to the Employee a further sum of £50 sterling, or its equivalent in local currency at the then rate of exchange, for outfit and expenses incurred by him meantime.

Passage money and outfit allowances repayable in certain circumstances

5. IF the Employee shall continue to serve the Company for the full period of four years hereunder or if he shall be dismissed by the Company for or on account of ill-health (unless occasioned by his own misconduct or wilful neglect), or on account of his incapacity (otherwise than through illness) as provided by Clause 11 hereof, the Company will make no claim nor shall the Employee be liable to repay to the Company the money so advanced by the Company for his passage as aforesaid or the said two sums of £50 each (or so much thereof respectively as has been paid), but, save as aforesaid, in all cases where the Employee is dismissed by the Company or shall leave the service of the Company before the end of the said period of four years without the previous consent of the Company he shall forthwith repay the said sums to the Company.

Remuneration

6. THE Company will pay the Employee from the date of his entering upon his duties as aforesaid and whilst employed at the Office aforesaid a salary for and during the first year at the rate of Rupees Nine hundred and twenty five per month

for and during the second year at the rate of Rupees Nine hundred and fifty per month

for and during the third year at the rate of Rupees One Thousand per month

for and during the fourth year at the rate of Rupees One Thousand and twenty five per month.

and if the Employee is required to proceed to any other Office of the Company or to any Associated Company as provided by Clause 2 hereof then at such rate as may be comparable to the salaries already paid to other Employees at such other Office having a similar length of service with the Company and its Associated Companies. Such salary shall be payable in monthly instalments on the last day of each and every calendar month. The Company will also pay to the Employee all expenses properly incurred by him whilst engaged in travelling on the business of the Company, including the cost of a passage should the Employee be required to proceed from one Office of the Company in the East to another, and, in the event of the illness of the Employee (other than illness which is the result of the Employee's own misconduct or wilful neglect), the Company will pay the expense of medical attendance by the Company's Medical Officer.

Compliance with rules of the Company

7. THE Employee shall, during the full period of his engagement, be and remain under and subject to the directions superintendence and control of the Resident Directors or Director or the Manager for the time being of the Company's business at the Office aforesaid or elsewhere in the East, and shall devote himself diligently faithfully honestly and exclusively to his duties and shall efficiently carry on and perform the same, and shall at all times use his best endeavours to improve and extend the business of the Company for the benefit and best advantage of the Company, and shall obey all lawful and reasonable commands of the Company whether given through the Resident Directors or Director or

2

113

the Manager for the time being of the Company's business at the Office aforesaid or elsewhere in the East, and shall at all times observe perform and be bound by all and every the rules and regulations for the time being of the Company whether contained in the printed book of Rules and Regulations to be observed by the members of the staff of the Company (a copy of which the Employee admits to have received) or otherwise.

8. THE Employee shall not, without permission first had and obtained, leave or absent himself from the Office at which he is employed unless for the purpose of executing the orders and directions of the Company or the Resident Directors or Director or the Manager of the business of the Company for the time being at the Office aforesaid or unless prevented from attending at the said place of business by ill-health.

9. THE Employee shall not at any time during the continuance of his employment or thereafter reveal or disclose any matter or thing respecting the business of the Company or its affairs to any person or persons other than the Company, and shall at all times make known and disclose to the Company all correspondence which he shall enter into carry on or receive in connection with the business of the Company with any person firm or company whomsoever, and shall not during the continuance of his employment either alone or jointly or in partnership with any other person or persons firm company or corporation whomsoever directly or indirectly, either by himself or his agent assistant or attorney or either in his own name or otherwise, carry on manage or be in any way concerned engaged or interested in any other duties business or employment.

10. IF the Employee shall be guilty of dishonesty insobriety or any criminal offence, or shall in any way misconduct himself or incur illness which in the opinion of the Company's Medical Officer is due to his own misconduct or wilful neglect, or shall become bankrupt or make any composition with or any assignment for the benefit of his creditors, or shall be guilty of a breach or non-performance of any of the covenants and agreements in this Agreement contained and on his part to be observed and performed, or if his ill-health should in the opinion of the Medical Officer of the Company unfit him for the work assigned him, then and in any of such cases the Company shall be entitled at any time thereafter to terminate this Agreement by immediate notice in writing to the Employee.

11. THE Company may, in the event of the Employee proving himself incapable (otherwise than through illness) of performing, to the satisfaction of the Resident Directors or Director or the Manager of the business of the Company for the time being at the Office aforesaid or elsewhere in the East, the duties assigned to him, terminate this Agreement by giving the Employee three calendar months' notice or in lieu thereof by paying him three months' salary, and also may, for any reason without assigning any cause therefor, at any time terminate and put an end to this Agreement by giving the Employee six calendar months' notice or by paying to the Employee six months' salary in lieu thereof.

12. AT the expiration of the said period of four years the Employee shall be entitled to leave of absence on full salary for a period of six calendar months (calculated from the date of leaving the Company's Office at which he is employed) provided that the actual date of commencement of such leave of absence be first approved by the Resident Directors or Director or the Manager for the time being

3

of the Company's business at the Office aforesaid, but such full salary shall only be granted on condition that the Employee shall return to Europe and shall refrain from work during such leave of absence ; and, in the event of his leaving the service of the Company and entering other employment during such period, he shall have no claim to any payment from the Company concurrently with the earning of remuneration from such other employment.

If it shall be mutually agreed that the Employee shall take his leave of absence before the expiration of the said period of four years the period of his leave shall be reduced proportionately on the basis of one month's leave for eight months' service, and if similarly it be agreed that his leave of absence shall be taken after the expiration of the said period of four years, then the period of his leave shall be extended proportionately.

Leave shall not be deemed to accrue from day to day and in the event of the Employee leaving the service of the Company for any reason no leave or allowance in lieu thereof shall be granted to him unless he shall have served the full period of the Agreement.

Return passage   13.   (a) IN the event of the Company terminating this Agreement in accordance with the provisions of Clause 11 hereof or under Clause 10 hereof owing to the ill-health of the Employee unfitting him for the work assigned him (such unfitness not being due to his own misconduct or wilful neglect) the Company shall pay the cost of the Employee's passage by air or sea as the Company shall decide from the Office aforesaid or elsewhere in the East to the United Kingdom if he departs for the United Kingdom within one calendar month from the date of such termination or in the case of ill-health within 14 days of being permitted so to do by the Medical Officer of the Company and in this respect it is expressly agreed and declared that time shall be of the essence of this Agreement. A certificate by the said Medical Officer shall be conclusive evidence and shall be final and binding on the Company and the Employee as to such permission and the date when it was given.

(b) AT the expiration of the said period of four years the Company will pay the cost of the Employee's return passage (by sea or air in accordance with the Company's regulations in force from time to time) from the Office aforesaid or elsewhere in the East to United Kingdom point of disembarkation and back provided that the Company and the Employee shall first have agreed that this Agreement shall, on its expiration, be renewed for a further term of years, and provided further that the Employee undertakes that, on the completion of such leave of absence, he will forthwith resume his duties at the Office aforesaid or elsewhere in the East ; but otherwise, at the expiration of the said period of four years, the Company will pay to the Employee the cost of his single passage (by sea or air in accordance with the Company's regulations in force from time to time) from the Office aforesaid or elsewhere in the East to United Kingdom point of disembarkation, provided he departs for the United Kingdom within one calendar month from the termination of this Agreement.

The Company shall be liable only for the actual cost of the passage used by the Employee. No allowance will be made towards a passage not actually taken or for a difference in fare if the Employee travels by an inferior class to that to which he is entitled.

Save as expressly provided by this Agreement the Company shall not be under any liability to pay to the Employee the cost of his passage from the Office aforesaid or elsewhere in the East to the United Kingdom on the termination of the engagement of the Employee hereunder nor shall the Company be or become chargeable in respect of the Employee in any manner whatsoever.

14. ON the expiration of six calendar months from the date of his entering upon his duties hereunder, and upon repayment to the Company, at or before the expiration of the notice in this Clause hereinafter referred to, of any amounts expended or advanced by the Company to the Employee for passage money and outfit allowances under the provisions of Clause 4 hereof, the Employee shall be entitled to determine this Agreement by giving the Company six weeks' notice in writing of his intention so to do, provided nevertheless that the Employee shall be entitled to seven days of grace from the expiration of the said period of six calendar months within which to give the said notice, but, if at the expiration of the said seven days of grace the Employee has failed or omitted to give the said notice, he shall immediately thereupon forfeit the benefit of this Clause.

15. IN the event of the termination of this Agreement otherwise than by effluxion of time, unless it be terminated under the provisions of Clause 11 hereof, the Employee shall not for a period of six months from its termination accept employment in any capacity similar to any capacity in which he shall have been employed at any time during the last three years of his service with the Company or any Associated Company of the Company from which he may have been transferred to the Company at any place within 900 miles of any office at which he shall have been so employed during the said period.

16. THE marginal notes hereto shall not affect the interpretation hereof.

5

116

IN WITNESS WHEREOF   JAMES BRUCE LEASK
on behalf of the Company and the Employee have set their hands to these Presents
in triplicate at   London   on the day and year
first above written.

Signed by the above-named

    JAMES BRUCE LEASK

in the presence of

in the presence of

of 1-4, Great Tower Street,
      London, E.C.3.

                        Witness.

For and on behalf of

HARRISONS & CROSFIELD, LIMITED

                          Director

Signed by the above-named

    PAUL GUNTON

in the presence of

of
Stonehouse Cottage
        Road
      S.W.18.   Witness.

Agreement to commence from
    9th July 1959.

        R.J. WATSON
    Manager.

117

HARRISONS & CROSFIELD,
LIMITED.

LONDON, CALCUTTA, CALICUT,
COCHIN, COLOMBO, DJAKARTA, MEDAN,
MONTREAL, QUILON, TORONTO, VANCOUVER.

CABLES & TELEGRAMS:
HARRICROS, LONDON.

TELEPHONE:
MANSION HOUSE 4333.

1 to 4, Great Tower Street,
London, E.C.3.

26th June 19 59.

REPLY TO Branches DEPT.

P. Gunton, Esq.,
Merthan Manor Farm,
Gweek,
Helston,
Cornwall.

Dear Sir,

Reservations have been made on your behalf on flight AI.116 which leaves London for Bombay at 15.00 hours on 6th July and on flight IC.159 which leaves Bombay for Cochin on 8th July. Your overnight stop in Bombay has been arranged by Air India at their expense.

You should report to the Airways Terminal, Buckingham Palace Road at 13.30 hours on your date of departure or direct to London Airport North not later than 14.15 hours.

We enclose your passport and also a copy of your agreement and we shall forward your airline ticket to you nearer your date of departure.

Your outfit allowance of £50 has been credited to your account with Barclays Bank, Great Tower Street, E.C. 3.

We shall arrange Personal Accident Insurance on your behalf in the amount of £5,000.

Yours faithfully,
HARRISONS & CROSFIELD LIMITED

Branches Secretary.

EXTRACT FROM "THE STORY OF TEA".

......, it is at this point that the romantic &
virtuoso figure of the tea-taster makes his
first appearance on the scene. These men by
long years of practice have developed their
sense of taste and smell to a pitch of sensitive-
ness that finds a parallel only among those orien-
tal musicians whose ears are so fine that they are
accurately attuned to quarter, eighth and sixteenth
tones.

TEA TASTERS THROUGHOUT THE WORLD USE A COMMON LANGUAGE TO DESCRIBE DRY LEAF,INFUSED LEAF (WET TEA LEAVES) AND LIQUORS. THE FOLLOWING TERMS REPRESENT AN EXCELLENT COVERAGE OF THE THREE IMPORTANT CHARACTERISTICS.

Tea Tasting Terminology

TERMS DESCRIBING DRY LEAF

BLOOM   A sign of good manufacture and sorting (where the reduction of leaf has mainly taken place before firing). A "sheen" which has not been removed by over-handling or over-sorting.

BLACK   A black appearance is desirable, preferably with "bloom". This term is used with Orthodox or Rotorvane manufacture.

BLACKISH   This is a satisfactory appearance for CTC and LTP manufacture teas, and denotes careful sorting.

BROWN   A brown appearance, with CTC and LTP manufacture, normally reflects too hard treatment of the leaf.

BOLD   Particles of leaf which are too large for the particular grade.

CLEAN   Leaf which is free from fibre, dust or any extraneous matter.

STALK & FIBRE   Should be minimal in primary or top grades, but generally unavoidable in the lower grades of an assortment.

GRAINY   Describes well well made CTC or LTP primary grades, more particularly Dusts.

EVEN   True to the grade and consisting of pieces of leaf of quite even size.

UNEVEN & MIXED   "Uneven" pieces of leaf usually indicative of poor sorting and not true to the particular grade.

FLAKY   Flat, open and often light in texture.

GREY   Caused by too much abrasion during sorting.

LEAFY   Orthodox manufacture leaf tending to be on the large or long side.

LIGHT   A tea light in weight and of poor density. Sometimes flaky.

MAKE   Well made (or not) and must be true to the grade.

NEAT   A grade having good "make" and size.

NOSE   Smell of the dry leaf.

CHOPPY   Orthodox (or Rotorvane) manufacture leaf which has to be cut by a "breaker" during sorting.

CHESTY   Inferior or unseasoned packing materials cause this taint.

POWDERY   Fine light dust.

TIP   A sign of fine plucking and apparent in the top grades of Orthodox manufacture.

WELL TWISTED   Applicable to Orthodox manufacture. Often referred to as "well made" or "rolled" and used for describing whole leaf grades.

'A character or taste foreign to tea'

'Well twisted'

TERMS DESCRIBING INFUSED LEAF

BRIGHT A lively bright appearance. Usually indicates bright liquors.

DULL Lacks brightness and usually denotes a poor tea. Can be due to faulty manufacture and firing, or a high moisture content.

GREEN Caused by under-fermentation, or characteristic of leaf from immature bushes (liquors often raw or light).

MIXED OR UNEVEN Leaf of varying colour.

AROMA Smell or scent denoting "inherent character"; usually at high elevations.

'Individual tasters have their own expressions, not necessarily widely used.'

'Tea left lying about'

TERMS DESCRIBING LIQUORS

BRISK The most "live" characteristic. Results from good manufacture.

BRIGHT Denotes a lively fresh tea with good keeping quality.

COLOURY Indicates useful depth of colour and strength.

CHARACTER An attractive taste when describing better high elevation growth, and peculiar to origin.

FLAVOUR A most desirable extension of "character" caused by slow growth at high elevations and comparatively rare.

STRENGTH Substance in cup.

QUALITY Refers to "cup quality" and denotes a combination of the most desirable liquoring properties.

CREAM A precipitate obtained after cooling.

FULL A good combination of strength and colour.

PUNGENT Astringent with a good combination of briskness brightness and strength. (More related to best quality North Indian teas).

DRY Indicates slight over-firing.

HIGH-FIRED Over-fired but not bakey (or burnt).

BAKEY An over-fired liquor.

BURNT Extreme over-firing.

DULL Not clear, and lacking any brightness or briskness.

FRUITY Can be due to over-fermentation and/or bacterial infection before firing. An over-ripe taste.

EARTHY Normally caused by damp storage. A taste which can at times be "climatically inherent" in leaf from certain origins.

GONE OFF A flat or old tea. Often denotes a high moisture content.

HARSH A taste generally related to under-withered leaf.

LIGHT Lacking strength and any depth of colour.

GREEN (or raw) An immature character. Often due to underfermentation (and sometimes under-wither).

PLAIN A liquor which is "clean" but lacking in the desirable characteristics.

COARSE Fibre content.

BAGGY A taint normally resulting from unlined hessian bags.

FLAT Unfresh, (usually due to age).

SMOKY Mainly caused by leaks around the dryer heating tubes.

SOFT The opposite of briskness and lacking any "live" characteristic. Caused by inefficient fermentation and/or firing.

STEWED A soft liquor with an undesirable taste. Caused by faulty firing at low temperatures and often insufficient air flow.

THIN An insipid light liquor which lacks any desirable characteristics.

WEEDY A grass or hay taste related to under-withering.

TAINTS (in general) A character or taste which is "foreign" to tea.

AFRICA TEA BROKERS LIMITED

Plantation House Nairobi P.O. Box 30464   Ralli House Mombasa P.O. Box 81883

1st April 1977

These teas of Formosa origin have been packed and exported to the U.S. and to Europe by Tait & Company. Ltd. since 1886.

Originally they were shipped by junk from the Tamsui River across to Foochow where they were loaded into the fast tea clippers and raced to Europe and the U.S. to be first on the market in order to command a higher price. Now they are shipped by modern freighters direct from Keelung to all parts of the world.

OOLONG tea is a speciality of Formosa. The whole leaf is dried, rolled, and gently cooked in baskets over slow burning charcoal. It has the flavour of ripe peaches.

JASMINE tea is sun dried without fermenting and is combined with the blossoms of the Jasmine flower to give it flavour. The flowers may be either served with the tea or removed before brewing.

LAPSANG SOUCHONG tea was originally grown and produced in certain districts on the Mainland of China where the soil contained a high percentage of shale oil. When brewed it was found that the leaf carried a slightly tarry flavour. This tea of acquired flavour became in great demand for making high class and exclusive blends and it is now made artificially and very successfully in Formosa by smoking the fired leaf with wet pine chips.

FORMOSA BLACK tea with Keemun flavour is more delicate than Indian or Ceylon teas and possesses a characteristic flavour of fine China tea.

TAIT & COMPANY. LTD.

TAIT & COMPANY LTD

A GLOSSARY PRINTED BY TAIT & COMPANY LTD,TAIPEI FOR INCLUSION IN THEIR CHRISTMAS PACKS OF TWO GIFT TEAS EACH. THE TEAS WERE PACKETED INDIVIDUALLY IN SILVER PAPER AND PLACED IN BETWEEN SPLIT BAMBOOS TO PREVENT THE LEAF FROM BEING CRUSHED IN TRANSIT. THE PACKS WERE THEN PLACED IN SMALL WICKER BASKETS SECURED WITH RED RIBBON.

A TEA DICTIONARY

ASSAM	SOUTH INDIA
1. Company Sahib	V. A.
2. Burra Sahib	Peria Durrai
3. Chotta Sahib	Chinna Durrai
4. Burra Mem Sahib	Peria Duraisany
5. Chotta Mem Sahib	Chinna Duraisany
6. Babu	Aiya
7. Head Tea House	Tea Maker
8. Sardhar	Kangani
9. Chowkidar	Kavulkaran
10. Plucking Table	Muttom
11. Flush	Impulse
12. Bhanji	Vungi
13. Decentre	Handle
14. Infills	Supplies
15. Recovery %	Outturn %
16. Coarse Mal	Bulk
17. Googies	Roll Breakers
18. Chotta Peg	One small
19. Cheers !	Cheers !

THE INDUSTRIES IN NORTH AND SOUTH INDIA HAVE THEIR OWN DISTINCT IDENTITIES WITH DIFFERENT WORDING FOR INDIVIDUALS ON TEA ESTATES, AGRICULTURAL CONDITIONS AND TEA FACTORY MACHINERY. HOWEVER, 'CHEERS' IS UNIVERSAL!

APPENDIX
SOUTH OF GOA

12500 4/57.

HARRISONS & CROSFIELD LTD.,
(INCORPORATED IN ENGLAND. LIABILITY OF MEMBERS LIMITED.)

TELEGRAPHIC ADDRESS:
"CROSFIELD" QUILON.

TELEPHONE NO. 652.

POST BOX No. 4,

QUILON, Jany. 4th, 19 69.
(SOUTH INDIA.)

REPLY SHOULD BE ADDRESSED TO

Management Department
HARRISONS & CROSFIELD LTD.,
AND NOT TO ANY INDIVIDUAL.

JNR: GJB.

P. Gunton, Esq.,

Cochin.

Dear Sir,

In accordance with Rule No.2 of the
General Rules of the Company, you rank
as a regular member of the Staff from
the 9th of this month.

You will then be entitled to receive
the equivalent of a further £50 towards
the cost of tropical outfit. Please
inform F. & A. Dept how you wish this
payment to be made. We attach a copy
of the receipt which the Company requires
in respect of this payment.

Yours faithfully,
Harrisons & Crosfield, Ltd.,

J.N.ROFE
MANAGER.

Encl.1.

"From ancient times no Master or Fellow could be absent from his Lodge, especially when warned to appear at it without incurring a severe censure unless it appeared to the Master and Wardens that pure necessity hindered him". *Antient Charges III*

YEAR OF WARRANT 1921.

LODGE COCHIN NO. 4359 E. C.

Wor. Bro. A. I. IPE
WORSHIPFUL MASTER

Cochin, 1st May 1964.

Bro. _____

Dear Sir and Brother

I am directed by the Worshipful Master to request your attendance at the Regular Meeting of the Lodge to be held at the "KODER HALL" Cochin, on SATURDAY 23rd May 1964 at 7 p.m. precisely'

The agenda of business is annexed

Yours fraternally,

M. A. CHACKO
SECRETARY
C/o. MESSRS. FORBES EWART & FIGGIS LTD., COCHIN-1.

LODGE OF INSTRUCTION Friday 22-5-'64. at 6 P. M.
Preceptor of Lodge of instruction
Wor Bro. S. S. KODER.

The brethren are requested to note the Antient Charges printed on the top of this page. Officers in particular must notify the Wor. Master if they are unable to attend a meeting

OFFICERS FOR THE YEAR 1964.

S.No	Reg No.	Date	NAMES	
14	181	24-10-'53	Wor. Bro. A. I. Ipe	Wor. Master
15	196	13- 8-'55	,, O. Thomas	Senior Warden
16	197	13- 8-55	,, A. Madhavan	Junior Warden
			,, ,, G. S. Rangaswamy	I. P. M.
17	✦209	19- 5-'56	,, K. R. L. Bandey P. W.	Chaplain
18	183	12-12-'53	,, E. S. Koder	Treasurer
19	192	23-10-'54	,, M. A. Chacko P. W.	Secretary
			,, S. S. Koder	Director of Ceremonies
20	✦221	23- 2-'57	,, G. J. Ancheril	Senior Deacon
21	237	22- 8-'59	,, D. A. Kamath	Junior Deacon
22	238	22- 8-'59	,, K. R. Viswanathan	Almoner
23	231	22-11-'58	,, J. W. Joshua	Organist
24	216	20-10-'56	,, D. B. Khona	Asst. Director of Ceremonies
25	250	21-10-'61	,, P. Gunton	Asst. Sec.
26	✦246	22-10-'60	,, K. Kurvilla	Inner Guard
27	245	27- 8-'60	,, G. K. Kuriyen	Steward,
28	247	19-11-'60	,, Achuthan Pillay	,,
29	256	24- 8-'63	,, M. C. Mathews	,,
30	✦254	17-11-'62	,, Alex George	Tyler
			MEMBERS	
31	✦ 92	J 17- 8-'40	Bro. V. K Arvindaksha Menon	M. M.
32	✦126	17-11-'45	,, J. H. Williams	M. M.
33	✦144	14- 2-'48	,, C. H. Mclean	M. M.
34	157	19-11-'49	,, V. B. Mohammed	M. M.
35	✦165	24- 3-'51	,, V. Mathen	M. M.
36	170	22- 3-'52	,, T. C. Varkey	P. W.
37	✦187	13- 2-'54	,, H. Norman	M. M.
38	191	23-10-'54	,, M. V. K. Menon	M. M.
39	✦194	21- 5-'55	,, V. Somasundaram	M. M.
40	✦198	17- 9-'55	,, A. V. Govindan	M. M.
41	✦199	17- 9-'55	,, Oonithon Thomas	M. M.
42	✦204	10-12-'55	,, J. I. Downie	M. M.
43	205	10-12-'55	,, A. R. May	M. M.
44	206	24- 3-'56	,, T. Bhose	M. M.
45	212	11- 8-'56	,, R. J. Chandy	M. M.
46	213	11- 8-'56	,, Thomas Joseph	M. M.
47	✦217	17-11-'56	,, D. E. Phelps	M. M.
48	✦218	17-11-'56	,, K. Newton	M. M.
49	✦223	22- 6-'57	,, T. V. S. Rajan	M. M.
50	226	J 18- 1-'58	,, R. M. Nair	M. M.
51	227	24- 5-'58	,, S. J. Asher	M. M.
52	228	J 30- 8-'58	,, P. N. Parashar	M. M.
53	✦229	30- 8-'58	,, M. C. Menon	M. M.
54	✦230	22-11-'58	,, C. T. John	M. M.
55	✦232	18- 4-'59	,, M. M. Mathew	M. M.
56	✦233	18- 4-'59	,, P. K. Ipe	M. M.
57	234	23- 5-'59	,, S. E. Koder	M. M.
58	235	28- 5-'59	,, J. E. Cohen	M. M.
59	✦239	24-10-'59	,, L. N. C. Jesudasan	M. M
60	240	24-10-'59	,, G. R. Hyde	M. M.
61	241	J 12-12-'59	,, S. D. Gamadia	M. M.
62	243	21- 5-'60	,, V. B. M. Bava	M. M.
63	✦244	21- 5-'60	,, T. S. Rajah	M. M.
64	249	22- 7-'61	,, H. N. Kamath	M. M.
65	251	18-11-'61	,, C. W. Steel	M. M.
66	252	J 18- 8-'62	,, A. Hutcheon	M. M.
67	253	J 20-10-'62	,, S. V. Kail	M. M.
68	255	20- 4-'63	,, J. Anandjee	M. M.
69	257	J 14-12-'63	,, N. S. Koder	M. M.
70	258	21- 3-'64	,, D. V. Bobb	E. A.

✦ Non Resident.

J Joined.

TOMMY AND PAUL

INVITE

TO A

BOTTLE PARTY

AT THE CHUMMERY

ON

FRIDAY 27th OCTOBER

AT

7-45 p. m.

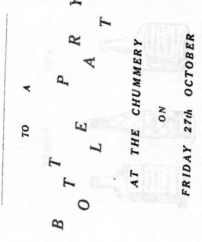

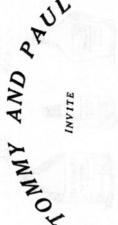

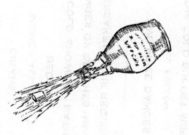

R I P

PRINTED AT THE SWARAJ PRINTERS, COCHIN-1

BRING YOUR BOTTLE

ANY SIZE

ANY SHAPE

WE WILL SUPPLY THE FOLLOWING

SODA

TONIC

LIME

ICE

CIGARETTES

CIGARS

MUSIC - ALL SORTS

BEDS

COLD SHOWERS / BATHS

CHANGES OF CLOTHES (MEN ONLY)

BREAKFAST - IF REQUIRED

———

TWO PRIZE DANCES

WILL FOLLOW

THE COLD BUFFET SUPPER

R. S. V. P.

DRESS:- BE COMFORTABLE !

COCHIN
GYMKHANA CLUB
1960

COCHIN GYMKHANA CLUB

OFFICERS 1960/61

President :

C. G. WATERS

Hon. Secretary / Treasurer :

P. GUNTON

Committee :

R. LUFF

H. BOWMAN

A. D. PEACOCK

Cricket Captain	—	S. Y. HOLLAND
Football Captain	—	G. McLEISH
Hockey Captain	—	M. E. BURBRIDGE

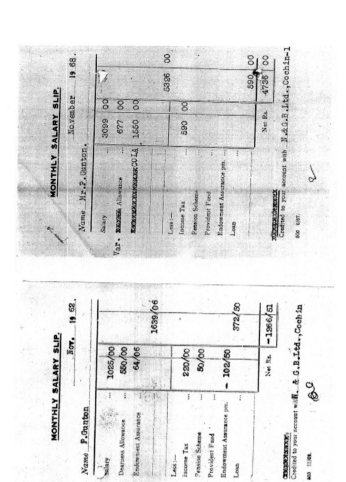

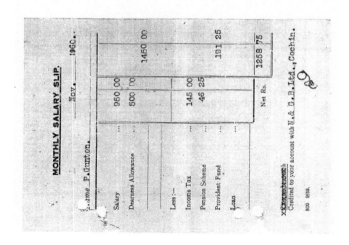

EXTRACT FROM BOOK 'LAND OF PERUMAL' BY MR. DAY   MADRAS 1860

BEGINNING AT 2ND PARAGRAPH   PAGE 120 OF CHAPTER IV

The first place at which the Dutch established themselves was on the Western Coast at Cambaya, as early as 1617; within 50 years this station was abandoned as unsuitable, together with those of Brodera, and Chircees, both of which had been taken possession of in 1620. At Ahmenabad, the Mahomedan Capital of Guzerat, they founded a factory in 1618, and retained it until 1744, but as it proved unremunerative, it was then evacuated, leaving only a few natives as tenants until more propitious times should enable them to return and retain it.

The Dutch possessions in Persia, established in 1622 as well as their other factories in connection with them, or near the Western Coast of India were subordinate to Surat until 1633, when the former were placed directly under the supreme Government of Batavia. Vingorla factory was established about 1655, but there were resident Dutch merchants there as early as 1641. The Portuguese having in 1640 shaken off the Spanish yoke in 1646 entered into a treaty with the Dutch in which it was stipulated that the latter were to have free access to ports of the former until 1656 and also to be received as friends in all their settlements; whilst each were to retain the conquests they had made.

In 1667 the various factories, and possessions in Malabar, and on the Western Coast, including those of Quilon, Culli-Quilon, Cranganore, and Cannanore were placed under the Cochin Command, that fortress having become the seat of their chief power in India. The reason why the Dutch desired territorial sovereignty has been alluded to in the previous chapter. Cochin formed a good position where no Native powers could molest them and having failed in their attack on Goa in 1660, they succeeded in taking Cochin in 1663,

The Dutch power being now firmly established in Cochin they turned their attention to removing everything they considered obstructive to their rule, their religion, or their convenience. After the town had been plundered, all property both public and private was sequestered by the Dutch Company. Any inhabitant who wished to leave the place, was permitted to embark for Goa, the remainder were obliged to take an oath of allegiance to the new power. The fort and houses were left standing as before, but the streets were re-named. The Romish Churches, with the exception of the Cathedral of St.Cruz or Santa Cruz, were destroyed, as the latter was required as a storehouse, more especially for sugar from Batavia, and Cinnamon from Ceylon, as well as nutmegs, cloves, iron, copper, cordage, rice, pepper and other articles; its tower was used as a flagstaff. The Church of the Franciscans was employed for the celebration of the services of the Dutch reformed religion.

The Dutch Government soon commenced entering into treaties with the neighbouring Native States. On March 22nd 1663 a treaty was concluded with the Rajah of Cochin who consented to become their vassal, and by which, according to Article IX "all Christians were placed under the protection of the Dutch Company", the Article stating that all are under the jurisdiction of the Company, and should any be guilty of misbehaviour he is amenable to the Company's laws. By a subsequent treaty dated February 25th 1664 also Article IX it was stipulated that those Christians who reside in the Rajah's territory should obey and perform their obligations to that Government as the Heathen do. Deputies were despatched to the Rajahs of Quilon, Culli-Quilon and other petty States, and treaties of friendship and trade entered into.

Within the fortress of Cochin, Roman Catholics were debarred from exercise of their religion: whilst their priests were banished, and warned not to enter its precincts in their canonicals.

No lay professors of that creed were allowed to sleep within its walls, or hold any office under the new Government until they had taken an oath that they renounced not only their King but their creed, and thus a number of hypocrites were gained over that the other churches no doubt were well rid of. All the Roman Catholics who did not apostatize, left Cochin and refused to have any mercantile transactions with its new rulers. The Governor soon perceived that an error had been committed, and unless some remedy were discovered, Cochin bid fair soon to have only the garrison and the officials as inhabitants. A compromise was effected with the Roman Catholics, and the Church of Franciscans was returned to them, but before long disputes arose, charges and counter charges were made, so another arrangement became necessary. It was then agreed that no Roman Catholic Church was to be made use of inside the Fort, but the members of that communion had permission to erect a new one at Vypeen, and to remove to it any of the internal fittings from the Church of the Franciscans, they might desire. On that Island the Church now standing was consequently erected, and dedicated to 'Our Lady of Hope' in it the Altar and the old screen from the Franciscan Church may (it is asserted) still be seen. The office holders were to be Europeans, Portuguese Eurasians and their legitimate descendants.

For those of us who have been fortunate enough to have a craft commissioned, the launching date is a leading mark in one's life and although my initial achievement was a very modest affair, I can remember the day clearly when my fourteen foot canoe was launched in Cochin harbour, the bow moist with a dram of whisky.

In July 1959, I had been posted by my Company to their branch on the Malabar Coast for a four year contract at the age of twenty and with a childhood spent on the Helford River, the sea was a very significant part of my background. I quickly adapted in my leisure hours to sailing the Company's 18ft. Naini Tai, a splendid Lynton Hope designed craft, complete with bamboo spars, and one of eight sailing under the colours of the Malabar Sailing Club. However, as an ardent swimmer as well, there was a problem, for in those days, the one swimming pool was situated six miles away in the grounds of the Malabar Hotel, built on Willingdon Island in the middle of the harbour. Admittedly, this island was connected by bridges but cars were beyond the financial reach of young bachelors in those days and for four years I cycled to the office, to the Club, to social engagements — hazardous in the extreme at times with people, cows, goats, handcarts, piedogs, rickshaws, general motor traffic to contend with, and, the rigours of the SW Monsoon bursting inland from the Arabian Sea.

The swimming pool taunted me until I realised that a canvas covered canoe was my obvious answer to traverse the Cochin channel and I threw myself into the project with gusto. I was directed to a boat builder in the heart of the Bazaar and although he did not communicate in English, (and had never seen a canvas covered canoe), with the help of a bungalow retainer, I was able to convey the general idea. The project progressed well, despite the Monsoon when the builder elevated his working platform above the surrounding floods, waterproof canvas arrived from Calcutta, as none was available in South India, and with no waterproof paint available either, I used my Helford River "fitting out" knowledge by painting in what I considered

the best available. Meanwhile, back at the Cochin Club bar, word of the project had reached the ears of the more elderly expatriots who were not enthusiastic — "wrong wood", "wrong canvas", "wrong paint" — were murmured over the pink gins and even more depressing, "the likes of us are not generally seen in canoes".

Petronella.

However, the great day arrived and practically the entire expatriot community came to witness the launching. The name "Petronella" was called, the whisky poured and she was lowered into the water. The maiden voyage of a mile with an active passenger using the second double paddle was a great success and for the next four years I have wonderful memories of the days afloat, to the Malabar Hotel on numerous occasions, sometimes under sail, to the offshore sandbanks at sunrise, to drives down the coast with Petronella on the roofrack to explore the Kerala backwaters further, to canoeing through the Cochin Club gates in the height of a SW Monsoon and mooring to a stout Canna Lily on the flooded lawns and on one occasion, arriving at the Malabar Hotel clad in white dinner jacket and black tie for an evening reception on the lawn — (the return journey was equally successful!) Halcyon days and a spin-off for the builder, for seven other people had Petronella copied, including two Czechoslovakians who were erecting cranes in the port.

When I left India in May 1964, Petronella was sold to a tea planter friend in the nearby High Range for us on the Mudpatty Dam at 4,000 ft. and I sadly saw her leave Cochin on a lorry convinced that I would not see her again. Indeed, a three month return visit to Cochin in 1968 confirmed my thoughts and my wife was content to hear my earlier exploits with interest but with no proof available.

However, in March this year I received the unexpected opportunity to return to Cochin, once more for a three month period, and whilst spending Easter on a tea

estate in the High Range, now almost devoid of expatriots, a friend casually mentioned that he thought "my old canoe" was lying on one of the Estates. On Easter Saturday, I followed up this statement and remarkably, there in a garage swamped with rubbish, but still on her original trailer, sat Petronella, somewhat tattered as the canvas had long since torn but with a frame that was still very sound. The Indian tea planter advised me that he would have to "throw her out" the following week, as he was being transferred to another Estate, but if I wished to have her, I was welcome to take her away.

The task seemed enormous, but so was the temptation and my host, a long-standing Scottish friend simplified the initial stage — "No problem" said he, "I will send her back to Cochin on a tea lorry", and so she returned. The journey had made her even more bedraggled for the wind had shredded the canvas further and lengths flapped idly as she awaited unloading at the office under the intense curiosity of numerous locals. I had her stored quietly away in a warehouse, for discussions were underway with some officers in the Indian Naval Base who had cheerfully agreed to "have a look at her". On the 5th of May, I was invited to bring her to the Base Repair Organisation, so loaded on to the roof rack, we proceeded. The sentry at the impressive gates was highly suspicious, but finally convinced, we entered the Base and after an inspection, and an agreed figure, Petronella was accepted into the BRO to be restored "to her finest original condition".

I was due to leave Cochin on the 26th of May and in the meantime, the local agents for one of the leading British Shipping Companies had approached the London office to enquire if consideration would be given to accepting Petronella "on deck" for their next UK sailing at the end of May. Time passed quickly, I was in regular contact with the Navy, the ETA of the ship was put back two days, but my date remained firm! On the 22nd of May, a call from the Navy confirmed that the work was complete, I did not tarry but only to find that the paint was still very wet, so she was gingerly carried outside into the midday sun. I returned the following Monday, 24th May, and loaded her on to the roofrack again, looking really magnificent with all the BRO officers and men gathered round to give her a farewell salute. I felt very humble as I drove out of the Base to the astonishment of the sentry and around to the shipping agent's office where still no word had been received from London. However, at this stage my driver's nephew arrived to paint her name, a job that his father had executed so well sixteen years previously, and almost as confirmation, news in the affirmative was received from London the following day.

I left Cochin on schedule and the Malabar Coast seemed distant once I was back in the City but I was soon brought back to reality when the shipping papers, confirming Petronella's presence en route to Avonmouth, arrived on my desk. A noted warehouse company readily agreed to clear her through the Customs and when I arrived to collect her from their premises, I found it hard to credit that this craft had come so far against such odds.

On the 3rd of July, my two young sons and I trundled her down the slipway of the Blackwater Sailing Club on her original trailer and before taking the water in this country, my wife renamed her with another wee dram. The initial voyage this year was as successful as the original, my sons are delighted with her and I am sure that they too will later recall memories of a craft that will have given them so much pleasure.

COCHIN HARBOUR REMEMBERED

TO	: MR. I.L. LEWIS	EXECUTIVE DIRECTOR, TEA COUNCIL LIMITED, LONDON.
FROM	: MR. PAUL GUNTON	TEA BROKERS CENTRAL AFRICA LTD., LONDON.

29TH APRIL, 1994

Dear Lloyd,

Two possible contributions for "Tales from the Tea Long Room"

COCHIN HARBOUR REMEMBERED

During my first contract of an unbroken four years with Harrisons and Crosfield in Cochin, in the early 1960's, my salary did not permit me to run a car, but I used my monthly rickshaw allowance of sixty rupees to purchase and maintain a bicycle and build a canoe.

One evening, American Export Lines held a cocktail party on the Malabar Hotel lawn to which I was invited along with many other tea shippers. The night was fine and clear and the tide, on the turn, was flooding weakly at 1830 hrs so I canoed the one mile across the harbour, from Fort Cochin to the hotel jetty, respledent in Red Sea Rig - black tie, white shirt, cummerbund, black trousers - to moor silently beside the jetty onto which I stepped, noiselessly.

A hush fell on the gathering and the American shipping agent stepped forward to greet me - "Jesus Christ?" "Not quite," said I, "Paul Gunton!" The party was a great success and I returned safely on the ebb tide, one of numerous enjoyable voyages on the Malabar coast.

With kind regards,

P. GUNTON
MANAGING DIRECTOR

APPENDIX
AOTEAROA   THE LAND OF THE
LONG WHITE CLOUD

TYNAN

TIPS

the strongest tea you can buy

TEA

TYNAN

TIPS

RUTLAND INDUSTRIES LIMITED, AUCKLAND, NEW ZEALAND

TEA

1/2 POUND NET WEIGHT

DIGEST

TEA

THE RECOMMENDED TEA

net weight 1/2lb.

To retain the exclusive delicate flavour of

DIGEST TEA

WARM THE TEAPOT · USE A COSY

GUARANTEE. Every packet of DIGEST TEA is guaranteed. Any out of condition packets returned are immediately replaced free. Postage paid

Know All Men by these Present

that

Mr. Paul Gunton

of

Boskenna Ros, St Buryan. Penzance. Cornwall. U.K.

has this day

visited the Northernmost Lighthouse in New Zealand,

the Land of the Long White Cloud,

and has become acceptable as a Loyal Member

of this Society.

Witness :

Keeper of the Light.
24th October, 1965.

MOUNT COOK NATIONAL PARK

Congratulations

This is to certify that

MR. P. GUNTON
is now an Exalted Member of the Unique
Order of PLANE SKI-DADDLERS.
This Diploma entitles the holder to boast
without reserve of the most exhilarating
and exciting ski-plane landing on the
Tasman Glacier, the largest icefield in the
Southern Hemisphere.

Given under our hand this 18th day
of APRIL 1965

Signed

The Tourist Hotel Corporation
of New Zealand

THE HERMITAGE,
MOUNT COOK.

Form 1 (Reg. 2)

N.º 3747 (New Series)

5s.

UNDER THE MINING ACT 1926

MINERS RIGHT, NEW ZEALAND

NOT EXTENDING TO MAORI CEDED LAND

To whom issued: *Paul Gunton*
(Full name)

of *Boskenna Ros, St. Buryan Cornwall*
(Residence)

Date of issue: *Sixth* day of *April* 1966

Date of expiry: *Fifth* day of *April* 1967

Receipt of the fee of five shillings is hereby acknowledged.

Dated and issued at *Arrowtown* this *6th* day of

April 1966

Ian S. Clarke

Warden [or other designation of Officer].

(Receipts issued by Government Officers for the receipt of Public moneys must be given on numbered official forms.)

143

Institute of Advanced Motorists
NZ Inc
P.O. Box ~~5372~~ Auckland
26421 Epsom

MEMBERSHIP CARD

PAUL GUNTON

has passed the Advanced Driving Test and has been elected
a member of the Institute.

VALID TO	WHEN COMPLETED BELOW
30 - 6 - 12	79

New Zealand

Advanced Driver

Quarterly Magazine of the New Zealand
Institute of Advanced Motorists Inc.

Summer/Christmas Edition
Number 2
December 2005

NEW ZEALAND LOCAL LINGO

"If some Members were seriously perturbed about N.Z.'s economic future a Minister of Religion brought light relief to others. A packed meeting of the Christchurch Branch heard the Rev. R.A. Lowe analyse the N.Z. character. "Because we are comparatively new people we are far too self conscious about men being MEN and women WOMEN. The New Zealand male is suspicious of art because he imagines it is effeminate to be anything but a philistine, and at

football matches women are regarded as outcasts and bound to look to the wrong direction. The reason why there are more New Zealand women who are good novelists than men is that New Zealand men are no good at English. N.Z males speak a strange, monosyllabic sort of non-language. For example, it is almost impossible to give any New Zealand man a satisfactory medical examination. If a doctor asks him to describe his symptoms, all he will be able to get out of him is, "I'm crook." "

APPENDIX
SERENDIB

G.M. TOPEN

PRINCE BUILDING
PRINCE STREET
P. O. BOX 69
COLOMBO, CEYLON.

14th May, 1971.

P. Gunton Esq.,
Tea Department,
H. & C. Mills,
Colombo.

Dear Paul,

    Many thanks for your letter of 14th
May and congratulations on being selected
as a Member of the Ceylon Sailing Team.

    Subject to any unforseen developments,
I certainly have no objection to you being
out of the Island from the 15th to the 22nd
June.

                    Yours sincerely,

147

A letter received from our Cook in Colombo, Mr. P. Panniah whilst we were on furlough with my parents in Devon.

Copy of letter

2.10.12,
Temple Lane
Colombo 3.

Dear Master, Lady & little masters,

Received your kind letter thanks very much. Here it's raining daily. Happy to here that Master, Lady, & little one's are keeping well.

We are looking after the Flat well. The step-ladder is inside the store room. Please write to Mrs. Rasmussen to give the Floor polisher & the step-ladder out & also to buy a polish tin.

We are keeping well. Hope little masters are also the same. Spend the holidays well & hope to see you'll soon. Convey my kind regards to Lady & little masters.

Yours obedient servent.

P. Parriah

THE COOK WE 'SAVED' FROM THE CURFEW!

Jury List No 9393

SC No 5

Heddorf.

बाल्ख

24, 25, 31/1 : 1, 2/2 : 13

B 63902 GOVT. PRESS, CEYLON.

No. 40
Criminal P. C. 1898, § 271
(M 16") 3/45

SUMMONS TO A JUROR

'Name   To' Gunton, Paul

Merchant

Harrisons & Crossfields Ltd

'Place   of' 12, Baur's Flats

Colombo 1

PURSUANT to a Precept directed to me by the Supreme Court of
the Island of Ceylon, requiring your attendance as a Juror at the
next Criminal Session at   Colombo

* Place   you are hereby summoned to attend at the said Session at *_Colombo_

at ten o'clock in the forenoon on the   _24_ th   day of
January 1972 next.

Given under my hand this _13_ th   day
of _January_   , 19 _72_

Fiscal. WP.

N.B.—Any claim for exemption should be made by letter to the
Registrar of the Supreme Court immediately after service

1961

Court No 4 February 19th - March 1st 1973
(Former)

J 92   GOVT. PRESS, CEYLON.

No. 40
Criminal P. C. 1898, § 271
(M 16°) 3/45

SUMMONS TO A JUROR

'Name   To'   Paul Grentar.

Merchant.

'Place   of'   Harrisar & Crossfield Ltd

27.   Queen's Rd.

Colombo 3

PURSUANT to a Precept directed to me by the Supreme Court of the Island of Ceylon, requiring your attendance as a Juror at the next Criminal Session at Colombo

6.40

(2)

*Place   you are hereby summoned to attend at the said Session at * *Calombo*

at ten o'clock in the forenoon on the   *19*   day of
February, 1973   next.

Given under my hand this   *9*   day
of   *February*   , 19*73*

Fiscal. W.P

N.B.—Any claim for exemption should be made by letter to the Registrar of the Supreme Court immediately after service

152

CEYLON SEA ANGLERS' CLUB

Treasurers:
CEYLON HOLDINGS LTD.

Telegraphic Address:
"SMERVIL"
COLOMBO

Telephones:
29201—29204

P. O. Box 146

Colombo,_____197__.

23rd August   3.

P. Gunton Esqr.,
C/o. Barclays Bank Ltd.,
3, Great Tower Street,
LONDON E.C.3.

Dear Sir,

Permanent O'Seas Membership

Reference the above subject we write to
advise you that your had been placed in the list
of permanent Over Seas Members. We had forwarded
the receipt in respect of the payment of subscrip-
tion fees, to M/s. Harrisons & Crosfield Ltd.,
which had not been received by you and a duplicate
receipt is enclosed herewith.

Trust that you will find this is in
order.

Yours faithfully,
CEYLON SEA ANGLERS' CLUB,
Ceylon Holdings Ltd.,

Accountant.

Encl.
KA/GP.

153

DUPLICATE

'YLON SEA ANGLERS' CLUB.

Received from...... L. Gardiner Esq.......

the Sum of Rupees...... Fifty only......

being payment of...... Subs. for '½ Overseas M/ship......

Cheque Rs. 50/-
Cash

197 .....

REVENUE

COLOMBO 20.vi.73

CE.No. 10767

No. 145b & 22/3/73 rfrd. C. original receipt

THE CEYLON SEA ANGLERS' CLUB
CEYLON HOLDINGS LTD.

Director.

Treasurers.

154

TEA TALES

SOOTHING CUPPA

An RAF pilot returning from Cyprus escaped with minor injuries after ejecting before his Harrier crashed near RAF Wittering in Cambridgeshire. He walked to a farmhouse and was given a cup of tea while he waited for the emergency services to arrive.

Odd Ode to a Colombo Tea Taster

When the Market has been good
That is, be it understood
Tea gets three rupees or more
Compliments will simply pour
From the Broker's happy lips
'Teas are black and full of tips
Clean and even – nicely made
BOPs a stylish grade'
Fannings too are useful size
(Just what the Persian Market buys)
'Infusions even – liquors bright
Everything's in fact all right,
Even stalky BM3
Is really quite a useful tea.'

When the Market takes a drop
All these nice allusions stop.
All teas now develop faults
Of the most alarming sorts.
Now no longer BOP
Is what it's supposed to be.

It is 'stalky – fibry – grey'
'Mixed – uneven', so they say.
As for stalky BM3
It can no longer sell as tea!
Infusions dull or black or green
Liquors the thinnest ever seen.
Teas will now take on a taint
Of Hessian, Onions or new paint,
And, in fact, you might as well
Just burn the stuff – so what the Hell!

After sunshine comes the rain
But the sun comes out again
And I'm sure that in the end
Tea will take an upward trend.
So in spite of all this fuss
Tea is just the stuff for us
Although 'It's dammed ridiculous'

TO   : MR. I.L. LEWIS   EXECUTIVE DIRECTOR
                                           TEA COUNCIL LIMITED, LONDON.

FROM : MR. P. GUNTON   TEA BROKERS CENTRAL AFRICA LTD,
                                           LIMBE.

29TH APRIL, 1994

THE
GENTLEMAN'S RETURN

During a visit to Meddecombera Estate in Sri Lanka a tale was fondly
told one evening of the retired planter who had started his career
there as a creeper and after thrity-five years, through the ladder
of appointment, had retired as the local chairman to take up a
position on the parent Board in London.

Within two years and in his new capacity, he returned to his old
stamping ground and requested on his first morning to be up for
muster at dawn and to tour some of the divisions. Some time into
the drive, and whilst passing through some lines, an elderly woman
rushed into the path of the landrover and salaamed enthusiastically.
The vehicle stopped and for several minutes the couple talked very
happily, in Tamil, before the vehicle proceeded, when after a minute
or two of contented silence, the vistor turned to his host and said
fondly, "she was a fine woman in her day."

With kind regards,

P. GUNTON
MANAGING DIRECTOR

158

APPENDIX
DOLDRUM YEARS

HARRISONS & CROSFIELD
LIMITED

ESTABLISHED 1844

CABLES & TELEGRAMS:
HARRICROS LONDON EC3
TELEX: 28806

TELEPHONE:
MANSION HOUSE 4333
EXTENSION

1 to 4 Great Tower Street.
London E.C.3.
REPLY TO Secretary's DEPT.
REF.

15th December 1967

P. Gunton, Esq.,

Dear Sir/Madam,

    I have pleasure in advising you of the Directors'
decision to give you a Christmas present of £25. -. -.
After deduction of income tax, the net amount is £17. -. -.
for which our cheque is enclosed.

        Yours faithfully,
    HARRISONS & CROSFIELD, LIMITED,

Secretary.

HARRISONS & CROSFIELD
LIMITED

ESTABLISHED 1844

CABLES & TELEGRAMS:
HARRICROS LONDON EC3
Telex: 885636

TELEPHONE:
01-626 4333
EXTENSION

1 to 4 Great Tower Street.
London, EC3R 5AB.
Secretary's
REPLY TO DEPT.
REF.

16th December 1977

P. Gunton Esq.,

Dear Sir/Madam,

    I have pleasure in advising you of the Directors'
decision to give you a Christmas present of £30.00.
Our cheque is enclosed for the net amount due calculated
as shown below:-

Christmas Present		£30.00
Less Income Tax	£10.20	
National Insurance	1.72	11.92
		£ 18.08

        Yours faithfully,
    HARRISONS & CROSFIELD, LIMITED,

NB. The Dates and the Amounts!

Copy of a letter from P Gunton to Mr. G.O. Peake:

Harrisons & Crosfield Ltd
Cochin Office
Kerala
South India17/5/ 76

Dear Mr Peake,

As an active golfer, I thought that you would be interested in the enclosed which was handed to me by the President-elect of the Ootacamund Club on Saturday evening. This gentleman was particularly interested to learn that I was a member of the Company that had played a significant role in the development of the Golf Course and I can vouch that the situation is indeed very beautiful.

With kindest regards,

P Gunton

G.O. Peake, Esq.,
M/s. Harrisons & Crosfield Ltd.,
1- 4 Great Tower Street,
LONDON EC3R 5AB

PG:WJN

HARRISONS & CROSFIELD
LIMITED

ESTABLISHED 1844

BRANCHES OR ASSOCIATED COMPANIES

UNITED KINGDOM, INDIA, CEYLON, WEST MALAYSIA
SINGAPORE, SARAWAK, BRUNEI, SABAH, INDONESIA
HONG KONG, TAIWAN, AUSTRALIA, NEW ZEALAND
U.S.A., CANADA, SOUTH AFRICA, RHODESIA
EAST AFRICA, MALAWI, NEW GUINEA

CABLES & TELEGRAMS: HARRICROS LONDON EC3
TELEX 28906
TELEPHONE 01-626 4333
EXTENSION

1 to 4 *Great Tower Street,*
London. E.C.3.

24th May 1976

P. Gunton, Esq.,
Cochin

Dear Gunton,

      It was thoughtful of you to send me with your letter of the 17th May the note about the Ootacamund Club. This makes very interesting reading. It sounds as if it is in a beautiful locality and at such an elevation I imagine you can play in temperatures and humidity which are not too unreasonable.

      One interesting feature is the reference to cross-country golf in 1915 and 1916 which no doubt was introduced as a diversion.

      It is, however, interesting to recall that the famous old course at St. Andrews originally came into being because the residents of the town occupied themselves on the way out to the harbour which was then on the Eden River by hitting primitive balls with primitive implements into holes in the ground. They repeated the performance in reverse on their way home in the evening.

      I am especially interested to note your comment that the Ootacamund Club finances are on an even keel. That is quite an achievement these inflationary days and is a constant problem for golf club managements in this country.

      With my regards,

      Yours sincerely,

G.O.Peake

162

A firm in Germany ordered coffee from an English firm, and while the coffee was en route a few bags split open making it possible for rats to nest in them.

The German firm sent the following letter to England.

Schentlemens,

Der last two pecketches ve got from you of coffee vas mit rattschidt gemixt.

Der coffee may be gute enuff, but der rat durds schboils der trade. Ve did receive samples vicht you sent us. It takes so much time to pik der rat durds from der coffee dat it's hardly wurt it. Ve order der coffee clean and you schipt schidt mixt it, it vas mistake ja?

Ve like you to schip us der coffee in vun zack und der rattachidt in anudder – den ve mix it to suit der customer.

Write blease if ve shouldt schip der schidt bek und keep der coffee, or if we shouldn't keep der schidt and schip der coffee back, or schip der whole schidden vorks bek.

Ve vont to do right in dis madder but ve don't like all dis rattachidt buzness.

Mitt much respects

FRITZ SCHIMMELPFENNG

Fortunately, I did not receive any claims during my brief period trading Coffee!

APPENDIX
LIFE ON THE COAST

Imperial War Museum
Lambeth Road London SE1 6HZ

Telephone 01-735 8922

P Gunton Esq
No2 Glebefield Road
Hatfield Peveral
CHELMSFORD
Essex

Your reference

Our reference

EXH/MGH/MB

Date

15 September 1982

Dear Mr Gunton

Thank you for your recent letter regarding a shell which you found on the
battlefield at Salaita Hill in Kenya.

From the details in your sketch it would appear that the shell is a shrapnel
round from a British 12 pounder gun. The service designation of this weapon
was the 12 pounder 6 cwt Breech Loading Horse Artillery Gun. Introduced into
service in September 1900 the 12 pounder had been relegated to a training
role with the Territorial Force in Britain by 1914, being replaced for active
service by the 13 pounder field gun. However some 12 pounders were still in
service with Colonial Units during the First World War.

The weapon had a maximum range of 6000 yards. The ammunition was of the
separate variety, consisting of the shell and a bag charge for the propellant
which was placed in the breech after loading the shell. Your shell was fuzed
with a No65 time and percussion fuze which could be set for delays of up to
30 seconds or for instantaneous detonation on impact.

There were two batteries equipped with 12 pounder guns among the artillery
supporting the attack on Salaita Hill on 12 February 1916. These were the
Calcutta Volunteer Battery (later 8th Battery) of the 4th Indian Mountain
Artillery Brigade, and the 1st Light Battery, South African Field Artillery
(later 6th Battery SAFA) and so your shell could have been fired by either of
these units.

The later operations at Salaita Hill on 9 March 1916, when the hill was actually
occupied after the German withdrawal, were supported by 13 pounder guns of the
SAFA, therefore the shell could not have originated from that action.

I hope that this information will be of help to you.

Yours sincerely

M G Hibberd
Department of Exhibits and Firearms

165

The Chairman and Committee
of the
Marlboro Safari Rally
The World's Greatest
Motoring Event

express their appreciation to

P. Quartus

for outstanding services to the event

_____ Paws - Len _____ Chairman

Date 19TH June 1982

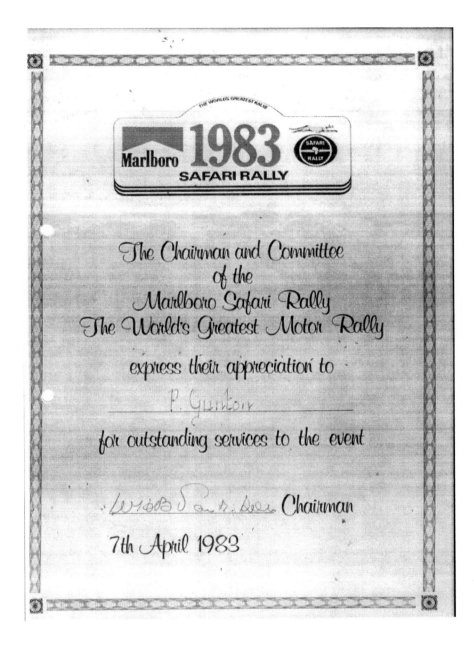

THE WORLD'S GREATEST RALLY

Marlboro **1983** SAFARI RALLY

The Chairman and Committee
of the
Marlboro Safari Rally
The World's Greatest Motor Rally

express their appreciation to

P. Gunton

for outstanding services to the event

W1983 .... Chairman

7th April 1983

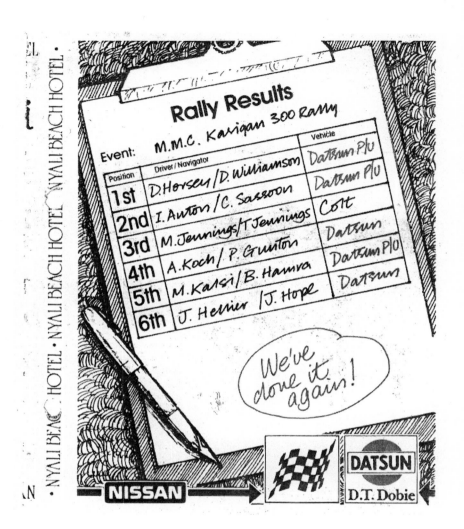

Certificate of Participation

Awarded for Completing a Mombasa Motor Club Rally

This is to Certify that

A Koch P Gunton

Driver/Navigator

has completed WIGGLESWORTH KASIGAU 300

and has attained FOURTH position overall

Certified this 12th Day of JUNE 1983

Clerk of the Course

INSTITUTE

OF

ADVANCED

MOTORISTS

(KENYA)

INFORMATION BOOKLET

'SKILL WITH RESPONSIBILITY'

Coastweek

MEMBER N.P.A. EAST AFRICA   G.P.O. REGISTERED NEWSPAPER

⊛ ENTERTAINMENT ⊛ NEWS ⊛ SHIPPING ⊛ COMMENT ⊛ SPORTS

Issue No. 2710 March 05 - 11, 2004.   PRICE - KENYA TWENTY FIVE SHILLINGS

'FAIR SAILING IN A STEADY WIND WITH FAST EBBING TIDE'

The fourth and final race for FEBRUARY MONTHLY MUG was sailed on Wednesday, the 25th by four boats in a steady fair wind with fast ebbing tide.

Osprey, TANTIVY, sailed by Scott McClelland, Susan Graham and Brian Emmott, were 2nd.

It was good to see Cecily and Paul Gunton, who were on holiday in Kenya from England, came to the Club and sailed with Barry Mitchell and Peter Mwangi in Osprey ATALANTA.

Half way the course Barry had rigging problem with the spinnaker losing valuable sailing time and finished in 3rd position.

Paul was a regular sailor and a member of MYC from 1978-1983 and Rear Commodore in 1980.

Steve Ogada in Topper STANRAY was 4th.

The three most enthusiastic sailors turned up to receive instruction from Steve Ogada who willingly stepped into the role of trainer.

[...] round the sailing area and the race course with Abdul Husain not far being in Airfoot.

Steve Ogada took the fleet out to Ishlia, Mtongwe, picking his way through numerous port movements and off to Likoni before heading safely back to the Club side of the channel where he ran the races.

• Sailing is an enjoyable sport where independence is gained, it is character and confidence building.

There is room for more

event.

The Juvenile Cup was also scheduled for the same day, but sadly there were no entries.

[...] crossing on the way to the second mark, Green Cable buoy saw Chanzo get into irons and lose out to Ishlia, the oldest helm in the race, who then looked all set to lead the way until she took a blistering tumble on the run back to Likoni.

In the meantime the fast boats were heading off from the start.

Cat's Paw, Sha Khan and Andy Burnard - the oldest by far accumulative age combination of helm, crew and boat took their first tumble before

passed Likoni Buoy, looked at the wild and uninviting waves and wind of the open sea on the way to Green Cable and decided discretion was the better part of [...]

Cat's Paw picked themselves up and dusted themselves down to continue with their race and to knock up several more capsizes which seem to have exceeded more than five, but one does tend to lose count.

Meanwhile the two Lasers continued to do battle rounding Likoni for the second time together, Ishlia having managed to right her boat and proceed ahead of Chanzo who was approaching fast.

Ishlia sailed away from Chanzo again, attributable only to a new sail, and continued to lead the fleet for another six marks before

torments as they went.

Up and off again, Ishlia not noticing yet another synchronized capsize with Cat's Paw heard an unwelcome ping on righting the mast and a torn sail !

The noise made heads turn and caused Cat's Paw to capsize in sympathy but they managed to sail themselves round the course to finish in third place while Ishlia, head hung, had to face the indignity of being towed home in the knowledge that the boom has to be replaced as half of it now resides in the bottom of Kilindini Harbour.

However the wind was up and the sailing was fun.

Michael Smewing and Ibrahim Khan claimed the trophy and Barakat Hashmani was present

APPENDIX
THE WARM HEART OF AFRICA

A letter from Fred – the Lake cottage watchman, who always experienced cash flow problems.

20/2/88

Please Sir,

Try to brow me K5.00 My Family has no food I will give you next week on 26/2

Yrs Security Guard

Fred

Request duly granted.

I was sailing our *Enterprise* sailing dinghy on Lake Malawi before sunrise on New Year's Day 1990 and having witnessed the dawn of a new decade, Fred was awaiting my return to the beach at 0545 hrs.

"A Happy New Year sir and please may I have a salary advance of ten Kwatcha?"

His request was happily granted on a beautiful morning and I completed my first business transaction of the decade.

The Government of the Republic of Malaŵi

request the pleasure of the company of

Mr and Mrs P Gunton

at the National Service of Worship

to mark the **Silver Jubilee** of Independence Celebrations

on **Sunday, 2nd July, 1989,** at Kwacha International Conference Centre

at 10.00 a.m.

R.S.V.P.

The Managing Executive
National Celebrations Council
Private Bag 26
Blantyre
Tel.: 620 411

DRESS REQUIREMENTS:

LADIES : Day Dress or
National Dress

GENTLEMEN : Lounge Suit or
National Dress

Guests to be seated by 9.00 a.m.
PLEASE BRING THIS CARD WITH YOU

P.T.O.

STAND D/O

The Government of the Republic of Malaŵi

request the pleasure of the company of

Mr & Mrs P Gunton

at the Kamuzu Stadium to witness the Celebrations Displays

to mark the **Silver Jubilee** *of Independence Celebrations*

on **Thursday, 6th July, 1989,** *at 9.00 a.m.*

R.S.V.P.
The Managing Executive
National Celebrations Council
Private Bag 26
Blantyre
Tel.: 620 411

DRESS REQUIREMENTS:

LADIES   : National Dress or
             Day Dress

GENTLEMEN : Dark Suit or National
             Dress

Guests to arrive by 8.30 a.m.

PLEASE BRING THIS CARD WITH YOU

[P.T.O.

SECTION B

The Government of the Republic of Malaŵi

request the pleasure of the company of

Mr and Mrs P Gunton

at the Celebrations Dance

to mark the **Silver Jubilee** *of Independence Celebrations*

on **Thursday, 6th July, 1989,** *at Shire Highlands Hotel*

at 9.00 p.m.

R.S.V.P.
The Managing Executive
National Celebrations Council
Private Bag 26
Blantyre
Tel.: 620 411

DRESS REQUIREMENTS:

LADIES   : National Dress or
             Long Evening Dress

GENTLEMEN : Black Tie or Dark Suit

Guests to arrive by 8.30 p.m.

PLEASE BRING THIS CARD WITH YOU

[P.T.O.

STANDID

GATE :D

The Hon. S. G. Demba, M.P.

Regional Chairman of the Malaŵi Congress Party for the South

requests the pleasure of the company of

Mr. & Mrs. P. Gunton

at the Inaugural Ceremony of 1991 Youth Week

by

His Excellency the Life President, Ngwazi Dr. H. Kamuzu Banda

Commander-in-Chief of League of Malaŵi Youth and

Malaŵi Young Pioneers Movement

at the Kamuzu Stadium in Blantyre on Sunday, 24th March, 1991, at 12.00 noon

R.S.V.P.
Secretary
Youth Week Inaugural Ceremony
P.O. Box 30387
Lilongwe 3

PLEASE BRING THIS CARD WITH YOU

DRESS
GENTLEMEN : Lounge Suit
LADIES   : National Dress
          Long Dress
                    [P.T.O.

176

THE DAWN OF THE NEW DECADE: NEW YEAR'S MORNING 1990

My first sail of the Decade was early on New Year's morning, but it was
prompted by events exactly thirty years earlier when I was living at Fort
Cochin on the Malabar Coast, South India. There, three of us after attending
the New Year's Eve party at the Cochin Club, had organised dug-out canoes
to take us off shore before sunrise to see the dawn of 1960 and this we
did, fishing, too, and drinking black coffee, although it was three cups
before Duggie appreciated that each had been laced, liberally.

That morning, I have never forgotten and thirty years later I decided to
spend New Year's Eve at our lakeshore cottage on the shores of Lake Malawi
with my dog, an old friend and his family and between us, a Hobie 14
Catamaran, two Enterprises and one Miracle. Mike and I had enjoyed some
long, exhilarating hours of sailing on New Year's Eve, with the Dart 18,
eventually coming ashore with some reluctance after sunset, when I suggested
that events I had experienced thirty years before, should be repeated.
This suggestion was enthusiastically welcomed but we were all so tired
that we slept from 2000 hrs - 2230 hrs when alarm clocks awakened us to
celebrate the New Year; again we retired at 01:30 hrs but when the alarm
clocks awakened us again at 04:30 hrs, and by this time a very confused
dog, Mike and I rigged one of the Enterprises and were afloat just as the
first streaks of daylight were creeping over Fort Mangochi, now in ruins,
but built to protect slave traders against the Protectorate administration.
Dawn and sunset are short periods near the Equator and by 5 a.m. daylight
was complete and a magnificent sight with twenty-six canoes around us in
the pale light and relected in the almost still waters. The sun rose at
0512 hrs bathing us all in its brilliant rays and by the time we returned
to the beach, despite the few clouds, the temperature must have climbed
at least ten degrees within half an hour.

There to assist us, though, was our night watchman, Mr. Juma Sukali who
having greeted us enthusiastically requested an immediate salary advance,
so with the necessary paperwork completed, I had concluded my first 1990
business transaction by 0545 hrs. Mike duly retired to bed but conditions
were so beautiful I had my first cold beer on the lakeshore verandah retiring
to bed again just before 0600 hrs but I was swimming by 0830 hrs and after
a hearty breakfast, I settled down to browse through the "Lake Nyasa Pilot
or Sailing Directions", (Compiled 1955-1959) a few of the entries of which
are so different and interesting from anywhere else that I have sailed,
that I have noted them as follows - remembering that Lake Malawi is the
twelveth largest lake in the World with Malawi, Mozambique and Tanzania
Coastlines, it is approximately 365 miles long and 52 miles wide and the
datum to which all soundings and heights are refered, has been taken to
be 1546.5ft above mean sea level at Beira, Mozambique:-

Introduction:

"The expressions "put to sea", "seaward", "at sea" etc have been used
deliberately. It is essential that the mariner should rid his mind of
the popular conception of a "lake." Apart from the facts that the water
is fresh and that the traffic conditions are not so dense as in certain
areas of the sea, the lake should be treated with great respect and normal
seaman like precautions should at all times be taken."

Page 6

Monkey Bay Dockyard - the Nkwasi, a cargo vessel of 295 tons and cargo
capacity of 200 tons, was completed in 1956 from parts prefabricated in
the United Kingdom. The slipway on which she was built has now been
dismantled.

2/...........

Cape Mclear lies at the north-west extremity of Domwe Island. It was named by Dr. Livingstone after the then Astonomer Royal at Cape Town.

Tumbi Island West (506 Ft.). The Island is thickly wooded and care should be taken on landing to avoid the irritating creeper known as the buffalo bean (mucuma pruriens) which abounds in certain areas.

Old Livingstonia site of the Church of Scotland Mission before Dr. Laws took it to Bandawe.

The Glengarry Hotel, with a number of chalets, now stands on this site. (Now closed). Close eastwards are the ruins of the old Cape Maclear Hotel. The BOAC flying boats used to moor off this beach when they used Cape Maclear as a base and the latter hotel was a going concern.

During the rainy season large clumps of reeds and sudd break away from the coastline, often altering its shape considerably, and towards the end of the rainy season, these clumps form floating islands of varying sizes.

Port Johnston (now Mangochi). There are several well appointed stores....and Gymkhana Club (now the Lake Museum) which contains the binnacle and wheel from H.M. Gunboat Guendolen, commanded by Commander E.L. Rhoades during the First World War. At the riverside end of the main street is a red brick clock tower erected to the memory of Queen Victoria.

Kajulu Creek. The water however is generally muddy and dirty and should on no account be used for drinking without first being boiled. In order to avoid mosquitoes at night, it is advisable to anchor at least three cables clear of the reed line where possible.

Nasanjo Creek. The whole area surrounding these creeks consists of dense swampy gound, the haunt of hippopotami and crocodiles.

Kota Kota, (now, Nkhotakota); until the 1890's it was a centre of the slave trade.

Kaombe River area - towards the end of the dry season north easterly or easterly winds, force five to six, frequently get up with great suddenness in the early morning, subsiding during the afternoon.

The village of Kapando, about eight miles north-west from Unaka Lagoon and near which there are hot springs.......

Old Bandawe....lies 2.3 miles south-south-east from New Bandawe. It was the site of a Church of Scotland Mission established in 1884 by Dr. Laws when he and his Mission moved from Old Livingstonia at Cape Maclear. All that remains at this site is a church still in use, and a neglected graveyard, where the comparatively young age (25-30) of those buried there is notable.

Page 68

Likoma Islands, (adjacent to the Mozambique Coast - the larger is only 2.4 miles from the nearest point on the mainland). St. Peter's Cathedral, a fine large building stands in the Centre of the Universities Mission to Central Africa Settlement at Chipyela.

Page 83

Liuli.   The bay is entered between Kuyu Point and the Sphinx.......a remarkable overhanging boulder at the north end of a small island, is so called because of its resemblance to the Egyptian Monument, particularly when viewed from the eastward from inside the bay.   The old German name for the bay was Sphinxhavn and up to the first World war, it possessed a slip where repairs were carried out to their gunboats.

Page 85

The Sphinx - it was close round this rock that the Commander Edmund Rhoades on the 6th August, 1914, sailed Guendolen into the bay to bombard the German gunboat, Herman Von Wissman, then hauled up on a slip for repairs.   The German Commander was most indignant, pulled out to the Guendolen in a small dinghy to protest, and was taken prisoner for his trouble.   The poor fellow had not heard that war had been declared; so ended the first naval action of World War 1.

Page 89

The Livingstone Mountains which reach elevations of over 8,000 ft in places, rise steeply from lake level, and continue to the head of the lake and beyond.

Page 103

Coast from Ruarwe to Cape Manulo - Close off this coast is found the deepest water in the Lake (704 Metres - or - 230 Metres below mean sea level).

One can never determine one's destiny but I hope to be fit and well to celebrate New Year's Eve in 2019, thirty years hence, and to welcome the dawn of 2020 - afloat.

PAUL GUNTON
COMMODORE, NDIRANDE SAILING CLUB
BVUMBWE, MALAWI, 30TH JUNE, 1990

179

This serves to confirm that

MR. P. GUNTON

in recognising the needs of the
disabled in the community
has been elected to
LIFE MEMBERSHIP
of
Malawi Against Polio

Date 26/6/1993

Signed

EXECUTIVE CHAIRMAN

Valid

DIRECTOR

For Atten. Esq.
Wilson Smithett & Co
30 July 1993

Awake at 05.40 hrs this morning due drums at neighbouring beer hall. Hope patrons not planning three day event.

Good weekend.
P Gunton

Tea Brokers Central Africa Ltd
PO Box 5543
Limbe
Malawi
Tel:640 192 Telex: 44149TAEABROKAMI Fax: 640 462

Wilson, Smithett & Co
Sir John Lyon House
5 High Timber Street
Upper Thames Street
London EC4V 3LS

30 July 1993

P Gunton Esq
Tea Brokers Central Africa Ltd
PO Box 5543
Limbe

8pm
Thanks for your fax this am:

MJB awake 04.30 hours with usual alarm call.

ATK awake 05.00 hours with neighbour's dog assaulting milkman.

IDHG awake 05.15 with fox attack on poultry run.

DAHB transit time ex Robertsbridge 06.30 to Cannon Street extended to 2hrs 30mins due delay caused by BR track and signal failure

Farewell lunch for Don Maclean of Haines after 45 years in the Tea Trade in UK 12.00 – 16.00 today.

17.30 hours eagerly awaited by all. TGIF

Regards

ATK

Relations with our major shareholder were good.

CHIWALE ESTATE,
P.O. Box 5247,
LIMBE,
MALAWI.

26th May, 1994

For the attention of Mr. Peter Matthews,
The Editor,
Guinness Book of Records,
Guinness Publishing Ltd.,
33, London Road,
Enfield,
MIDDLESEX EN2 6DJ.

Dear

PHILODENDRON PLANT

At the request of Mr. Paul Gunton, Managing Director of Tea Brokers Central
Africa Limited, P.O. Box 5543, Limbe, Malawi I measured their impressive
green plant this morning that has been flourishing in the entrance hall
of their offices for several years and certainly since before Mr. Gunton's
arrival in 1986. We feel that this plant, growing from a small pot, may
qualify for an entry in your next edition of "The Guinness Book of Records"
and I confirm the lengths of my exact twenty-eight measurements as follows
- (there were several small loops and angles that could not be measured
so the total length is, infact, approximate).

HEIGHT 230 CMS X 4   920 CMS

1)	Length 265	265	15)	Length 175 CMS			175
2)	Length 350	350	16)	Length 130 "			130
3)	Length 380	380	17)	Length 135 "			135
4)	Length 345	345	18)	Length 65 "			65
5)	Length 225	225	19)	Length 400 "			400
6)	Length 318 X 3	954	20)	Length 198 "			198
7)	Length 140 X 2	280	21)	Length 130 "			130
8)	Length 55	55	22)	Length 120 "			120
9)	Length 146 X 2	292	23)	Length 110 "			110
10)	Length 75 X 2	150	24)	Length 144 "			144
11)	length 270	270	25)	Length 110 "			110
12)	Length 278	278	26)	Length 275 " X 4			1100
13)	Length 250	250	27)	Length 990 " X 4			3960
14)	length 160 X 3	480					
	Lengths	4574					6777
	Height	920		Pot Measurements:-			
	Total length from Pot	12271 CMS		Diameter: 22cms Depth 28CMS			

Mr. Gunton will be forwarding this letter to you together with a photograph
and we shall be most interested to receive your reply in due course.

Yours faithfully,

V. HENDERSON (MRS)
CHAIRMAN, THYOLO GARDEN CLUB, THYOLO

MALAWI

Black, Choice & Rosy

TEA

THE origins of the Malawi tea industry can be traced back to the experiments of Jonathan Duncan, a gardener at the Church of Scotland Mission in Blantyre, with tea brought from the Botanical Gardens, Edinburgh in 1878. Regrettably, the experiment failed but in 1886 another parcel of tea seed was brought by Dr. Emslie a missionary doctor on his way from Scotland to Livingstonia and additional seeds were obtained from London's Kew Gardens. Two bushes survived for the infant industry.

In 1891, Henry Brown, a former Ceylon planter, saw that Mulanje's acid soil and high rainfall offered very similar conditions to those

Malawi is one of the world's largest tea producers and to prove it each year buyers from over sixty tea importing countries converge on one small tea auction room in Malawi's Southern Region. There they compete for the right to buy Malawi's choice black tea.

Paul Gunton looks at the growth of Malawi's tea industry from pioneering days to present success.

in Ceylon and encouraged by this purchased seeds from Duncan and planted them on his own property, Thornwood, and nearby Lauderdale – both properties that contribute significantly to Malawi's tea production today.

From those pioneering days, tea cultivation in the Mulanje district developed followed by the Thyolo district and much later, on a smaller scale, Nkhata Bay district. Today the highly sophisticated industry has doubled its made tea production over the past two decades from 18.7 million kilograms in 1970 to a record 40 million in 1991. The importance placed on the quality of the crop has increased considerably. Malawi teas were previously used by blenders and packers for purposes of cost reduction when combined with teas from other origins but the emphasis now is on producing fine quality tea with the rosy liquors sought after by buyers worldwide.

In July 1965 a tea broking company was established known as Tea Brokers (Central Africa) Ltd. The first-ever lot of Malawi tea to be auctioned came under the hammer on the 17th December 1970 . Many buyers worldwide subsequently appointed agents in Malawi to purchase their regular requirements and as a result the Tea Auction is now one of thirteen world centres. Auctions are held bi-monthly from July to September (when yields are low) and for the rest of the year, ekly on each Tuesday morning. In 1984 a second tea broking company was formed, Tea and Coffee Brokers Ltd and in 1990 both broking companies catalogued a total of 464,801 packages selling 20.4 million kilograms – the auction held on the 1st May 1990 selling an individual record of 23,800

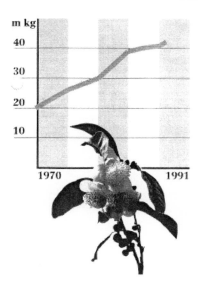

packages. Additionally, in a further encouraging development, tea producers in Mocambique, Zambia and Zimbabwe entrusted and sold tea through the auctions in the catalogues of Tea Brokers (Central Africa) Ltd.

In 1970 the Tea and Coffee Merchants Association was formed to provide a means of communication between the buyers and its counterpart organization, the Tea Association of Malawi Limited. This association now has twenty members,

comprising producers and merchants, local tea packing companies, small and large local exporters and multinational organisations. Stringent rules governing sales of Malawi tea are firmly established and prospective exporters must qualify before operating in auction. Although small by international standards, the auctions are very competitive with an estimated total of more than 60 overseas buyers represented in the room. Shipments to many worldwide destinations are trucked and shipped promptly after purchase. They often reach their destination before teas shipped from other countries with their own seaports, the fruit of successful cooperation between growers, exporters, freight agents and shipping lines. The principal importing countries for Malawi tea are the United Kingdom, South Africa, the Netherlands, the United States., Canada and Pakistan.

Ndirande Sailing Club

P.O. Box 2025
Blantyre

NLW/den

30 September 1994

Mr. P. Gunton
Managing Director
Tea Brokers Central African Ltd
P.O. Box 5543
LIMBE

Dear Paul

LIFE MEMBERSHIP

Thank you for your letter dated 1 September 1994 in the
above regard, I regret the delay in replying however initially
I was away on leave and upon my return I deemed it prudent to
convene a full committee meeting to finally ratify your
appointment.

I therefore now have great pleasure in confirming that you
have been granted life membership of the Ndirande Sailing Club,
which honour has been bestowed in recognition of the many
years of unselfish and hard work you put in as Club Commodore.

On behalf of both myself and the Committee I proffer our hearty
congratulations.

With kind regards.

N L WILLIAMS
COMMODORE

Committee

N. Williams.   P. Killick.   R. Mennell.   S. Mennell.   E. Tarleton.   Mike Denn.
E. Campbell.   C. Bailey.   P. Bailey

Insurance

Should you wish, DHL Tea-X-Press offers you the option to insure your tea samples at a nominal rate.

Investment

Using DHL Tea-X-Press to deliver your choice tea samples to international buyers is one of the best investments you ever make.

The cost of sending your samples will be negligible when compared with the resulting export orders.

How to book

your DHL

TEA-X-PRESS

Collection

Your local Worldwide Parcel Express consultant will ensure personalised attention at all times.

To book your collection, simply call your nearest DHL office and we'll do the rest.

We keep your promises

PHOTOGRAPH FOR INCLUSION IN THE DHL   TEA-X-PRESS PAMPHLET

INDEPENDENT ORGANIC INSPECTORATE

Weston Green Barn, Weston Colville, Cambridge CB1 5NS

Tel: 0223 290767   Mobile: 0850 632308   Fax: 0223 290143

P Gunton Esq
Tea Brokers Central Africa Ltd
P.O.Box 5543
LIMBE
Malawi

9th February 1995

Dear Paul,

It was good to meet you when I visited Blantyre recently and I am
glad that we could talk through the work you are doing for the
administration of organic produce. We very much hope that you
will continue to do this as you are doing an excellent job in co-
ordinating the various growers and their selection of products.
You have now done this for three years and it would important
if you could try and continue to fit this work in.

During my inspections, I found a growing enthusiasm for ~~growing~~
organic produce and I hope that Europe will be a good market for
the grower.

I look forward to seeing you next year and many thanks again
for your help.

Yours sincerely,

Nigel Agar.

A DIVISION OF NIGEL S. AGAR & ASSOCIATES
Fellow of British Institute of Agricultural Consultants and Member of Association of Independent Crop Consultants
BASIS Registered 0/45 AC   VAT No. 373 2431 66

WINTER FLOWER SHOW   ST. JOSEPH'S LILIES

BLANTYRE CITY GARDEN CLUB

DATE 16. 9. 95   CLASS A 21

First Prize

NAME R. GUNTON

BLANTYRE PRINT AND PACKAGING

WINTER FLOWER SHOW · ROSES · THREE BLOOMS ONE

COLOUR - RED

BLANTYRE CITY GARDEN CLUB

DATE 16. 9. 95   CLASS A37

Third Prize

NAME R. GUNTON

BLANTYRE PRINT AND PACKAGING

SUMMER FLOWER SHOW : DAHLIAS : CACTUS : SPECIMEN OVER 6"

BLANTYRE CITY GARDEN CLUB

DATE 17-2-96   CLASS A 14

First Prize

NAME T.S.C.A.

BLANTYRE PRINT AND PACKAGING

BLANTYRE CITY GARDEN CLUB
PO BOX 1791 BLANTYRE
NOVEMBER NEWSLETTER 1996.

****

CHAIRMAN	DAVE CORNELIUS	642 282	ELAINE DAVIES	643 881
VICE CHAIRMAN	CAROL VARNDELL	642 167	ARTHUR SCHWARZ	642 723
SECRETARY	DAVID LUKA	662 206	MARIUM MUKADAM	640 912
TREASURER	SOPHIE WESTROP		GILL GIBBONS	
NEWSLETTER	SHIRLEY HOWLIN	533 281	ASST TREASURER PAT ROYLE	662 256

Dear Member,

This the first Newletter since the AGM and shows your new Committee above for the coming year.

Now we are about to go on a journey from Malawi to Ireland !!
I received a letter from Paul Gunton of Tea Brokers Malawi Ltd on a little exercise he undertook in August this year on the request of his wife Cicely and he very rightly thought it would make an interesting item for our Newsletter

BVUMBWE TO BALLYMOTE
****

"Cicely flew home ahead of me on leave to prepare for a family wedding in the West of Ireland on August 26th. I was bidden to bring some flowers from our garden in Bvumbwe, when I flew on the 22nd –a daunting prospect for I am no gardener and there was already some hand luggage accumulating. However Chrystal Hawkin gave me some invaluable advice and at sunset on 21st August I stalked round the garden and as requested picked the following varieties Arum Lilies 32, Anthuriums 7, and Strelitzia 5.
Their stems were again cut under water and soaked overnight in two buckets.
To catch the 08.30 hrs flight I was up early to pack them in an open cardboard box measuring 24 x 12 x 8 inches. A thick envelope was placed in the bottom and then a layer of foam chips. Each stem was individually wrapped in soaked tissue paper- -Strelitzia at the bottom, Arums in the middle and Anthuriums on the top. With no damage done the flowers travelled in the hold to Lilongwe and during my day in Lilongwe all flowers were unpacked and placed in buckets of water before being repacked for the flights to Amsterdam and London in the cabins
The box raised considerable interest throughout the journey and every hour or so I flicked in water and at one stage my regular requests for a glass of water prompted my KLM Hostesses to enquire if I was diluting my beers!!
Immediately on arrival at our home in England the flowers were unpacked and placed again in buckets of water to be repacked the following morning for the flight to Ireland, again in the cabin and flicked regularly with water.
At the final destination the flowers were placed in further buckets of water and arranged by Cicely the next day amongst other flowers.
The Survival Rate was good--only 6 Arum Lilies had to be discarded and when we left after ten days all the Strelitzia and Anthuriums were still giving the family much pleasure. The exercise was considerable but all the effort was far outweighed by the joy it gave the lovely bride and the family and guests who all expressed their deep admiration. A exercise well worthwhile"

Mr Gunton did enclose four splendid photos of the flowers in floral arrangements which I had to return to him. Such a shame you can't all see them. I really take my hat off to him because he must have been like an anxious father with 44 new born babies to keep alive!! No wonder he needed beers throughout the night! Congratulations Mr Gunton you will cope loike an old hand if asked to do it again and you must have a sense of humour to agree to such an undertaking!

Ready line

Ready line

*
/ '149 TEBROCA MI*
4=149 TEBROCA MI
6-811 TILDC MO
TO: MR. PAUL GUNTON
FM: MR. A.P. CAPUCHO PAULO   DATE: 30.10.96

WE THANK YOU FOR YR TLX, IT WON'T BE NECESSARY TO BRING ANYTHING BUT
GOOD SPIRIT OF AN AFRICAN ADVENTURE. DR. JO%O RIBAS AWAITS YOU AT
GURUE AND HE SENDS A MESSAGE THAT YOU'LL BE MOST WELCOME.

BEST REGARDS
A.P. CAPUCHO PAULO
*
44149 TEBROCA MI
6-811 TILDC MO...
30-10-96 10:27

(ssage: 163D-** received   On 30/10/96 at 10 h 21 Elapsed : 01 mn 38
Di connect code : 13

192

TEA BROKERS CENTRAL AFRICA LTD.

P.O. Box 5543,   Tel.: 640 192
LIMBE,
MALAWI.   Telex 44149 TEABROCA MI
                              Fax: 640 462

FOR YOUR INTEREST   28TH OCTOBER, 1998

At the invitation of Joao Ferreira Dos Santos, I paid my second visit to Cha de Magoma last weekend and was amazed at their progress and that of Mozambique, since my previous visit in November 1996. My two travelling companions included the wife of the Mozambique Consul in Blantyre and at the newly refurbished border post in Milange, we were welcomed and the formalities completed within minutes.

The road to Garue has been virtually rebuilt by a South African Company with World Bank funds and the journey that took us over six hours in 1996 was completed in just over two hours on Friday. En route, the local people waved and smiled as we passed - they ran away before - and arriving in Garue, the town was "alive", with people sitting on chairs outside cafes drinking beers in the afternoon sunshine. We did likewise and even the dogs were as relaxed, lolling against steps and scratching lethargically from time to time.

We dropped our lady friend with some friends in town and then drove half an hour to the estate to be welcomed by our Portuguese hosts who were as hospitable as before. We started early on Saturday with a tour of the estate that had been abandoned for eighteen years during the civil war. Only two hundred hectares now remain to be cleared, some of the vegetation being over twenty feet high, so it is not surprising that in areas most recently cleared there are numerous vacancies amongst the hard pruned bushes. However, with a background of hills, not unlike Mulanje, there is an adequate water supply to run turbines and the nursery beside a healthy stream, is stocked with over 200,000 seedlings ready for replanting.

Luso factory has been in commission for two years and will commence this season's production on November 1st and work on the war ravaged Monte Branco factory is almost complete, with roof replaced, troughs built, machinery installed etc and combined production is estimated at 1,000,000 kilos this season. However, Mulacala factory is beyond repair and is a complete wreck - as are many houses on the estate.

After a really interesting day and a fine luncheon and supper our younger host suggested that we see Garue by night and we gravitated to the Domino nightclub for a few hours. We were the only Europeans in the packed establishment but we were greeted warmly and the atmosphere like the new Mozambique was relaxed and happy with good music and ice cold canned South African beer.

It was with some reluctance that we drove back on Sunday, having collected the Consul's wife, but before we crossed the border we tarried for a snack in Milange, rather than drive half an hour to the Mulanje Club. Mozambique, though is on the "up" in more ways than one, greatly influenced by the hugh road improvements now permitting people to move easily around the Country without fear and oppression - a great step forward.

CONFIDENTIAL

Ref. No. CID/FBP/1/10/111.

Telegrams: CIDPOL LILONGWE
Telephone: 731 999

OFFICE OF THE INSPECTOR GENERAL
CRIMINAL INVESTIGATION DEPARTMENT
MALAWI POLICE
PRIVATE BAG 305
CAPITAL CITY
LILONGWE 3

21ST NOVEMBER, 1998.

TO WHOM IT MAY CONCERN

This is to certify that no convictions are recorded against:

...... MR. PAUL GUNTON ....

at this Headquarters, nor is anything known to his/her detriment.

G.L. NAKARI, A/SUPT.
for Inspector General

2ND IN CHARGE
C.R.O. AND F.P.B. CRIMINAL
INVESTIGATION DEPARTMENT

2 1 NOV 1998

PRIVATE BAG 305
CAPITAL CITY, LILONGWE 3

M. P. 0071/654/7.97

194

I.T.F. 109

INSPECTOR OF TAXES
P.O. BOX 250
BLANTYRE
MALAWI

MALAWI GOVERNMENT

DEPARTMENT OF TAXES №̲ ⎯40607

CERTIFIED THAT (FULL NAMES) MR. PAUL GUNTON

of TEA BROKERS C. AFRICA LTD BOX 5543 LIMBE

has made satisfactory arrangements for the discharge of his/her Income Tax obliga-

tions to the ~~date~~ of his/her departure from Malaŵi on 31 — 12 — 98

DEPARTMENT OF TAXES
ASSESSMENT OFFICE

24 NOV 1998

P.O. BOX 250, BLANTYRE

for _____
Inspector of Taxes

NOTE: This certificate is issued for the convenience of taxpayers and it in no way relieves or ex-empts any taxpayer from any of the provisions of the Taxation Act.

I.T. 100761/1MP/12.90

195

VOICE MATCHED

Now we wouldn't want to accuse Zambian tennis player Lighton Ndefwayl of being a sore loser, but this is what he said when he lost a match to his rival Musumba Bwayla (as quoted in New York's *Village Voice* recently and sent in by a *Lai See* reader):

"Musumba Bwayla is a stupid man and a hopeless player. He has a huge nose and is cross-eyed. Girls hate him. He beat me because my jockstrap was too tight and because when he serves, he farts, and that made me lose my concentration, for which I am famous throughout Zambia.

Lai See

Sadly we did not meet these two tennis players during our seventeen years in Africa.

LIMBE AUCTION No 34   1. 5. 90   TBCA   16580
                                      TCB   720
                                            23800

THE TEA BROKERS ASSOCIATION OF LONDON

SALE NO. 870

MONDAY, 30TH APRIL, 1990.

KENYA, UGANDA, TANZANIA, BURUNDI, RWANDA, MALAWI, ZIMBABWE,
SRI LANKA.

10.30 A.M.

	Catalogues	Breaks	Packages
1. Wilson, Smithett & Company.	1 2	101 9	5,360 260
2. George White & Company.	1 2	54 6	2,757 120
3. Thompson Lloyd & Ewart.	1 2	123 16	5,620 360
4. Haines & Company (London) Ltd.,	1 2	36 3	1,640 80
		348	16,197

LONDON   CIF   AUCTION   5 800
LONDON   FOB   AUCTION   1 620
                         23 617

BT.
OOGW

The week that the LIMBE TEA AUCTION offered
the Trade a larger quantity than in London

LONDON TEA AUCTION DETAILS

197

TEA BROKERS CENTRAL AFRICA LTD.

P.O. BOX 5543, LIMBE, MALAWI.

Telephone BLANTYRE : 640 344
Fax No. 640 462

Telex: 44149 TEA BROCA MI

<u>AUCTION NO. 18</u>

<u>TO BE HELD ON TUESDAY, 17TH DECEMBER, 1991</u>

<u>AT 0930 HOURS</u>

<u>IN THE BOARDROOM OF THE TEA ASSOCIATION OF MALAWI LTD, BLANTYRE</u>

<u>200</u> PACKAGES, <u>ZIMBABWE</u> TEA, <u>14,080</u> KILOS

<u>4</u> LOTS NOs 1 TO <u>4</u>

<u>600</u> PACKAGES <u>ZAMBIA</u> TEA <u>36,800</u> KILOS

<u>4</u> LOTS NOs 5 TO <u>8</u>

<u>2,800</u> PACKAGES <u>MALAWI</u> TEA <u>158,960</u> KILOS

<u>73</u> LOTS NOs 9 TO <u>73</u>

MALAWI COFFEE
<u>150</u> BAGS <u>9000</u> KILOS <u>1</u> LOT

<u>UNLESS OTHERWISE STATED, TEAS ARE PACKED IN SACKS/FOIL</u>

ORDER OF SALE

(1)   TEA   AND   COFFEE   BROKERS   LIMITED

(2)   TEA BROKERS CENTRAL AFRICA LIMITED

TO BE SOLD UNDER THE USUAL CONDITIONS OF SALE

LOTS MARKED X ARE LYING ON ESTATE AND WILL BE SOLD EX ESTATE.

TO BE DELIVERED TO TBCA APPROVED WAREHOUSE.

ALL OTHER LOTS WILL BE SOLD EX WAREHOUSE.

LOTS MARKED A ARE LYING AT AMI WAREHOUSE LUCHENZA.

LOTS MARKED B ARE LYING AT TACA WAREHOUSE LUCHENZA.

LOTS MARKED C ARE LYING AT MANICA STADIUM ROAD, BLANTYRE.

LOTS MARKED D ARE LYING AT MANICA WAREHOUSE LUCHENZA.

LOTS MARKED E ARE LYING AT LEOPOLD WALFORD WAREHOUSE, BLANTYRE.

LOTS MARKED I ARE LYING AT A.M.I WAREHOUSE, BLANTYRE.

DAY OF SETTLEMENT
30TH DECEMBER, 1991

LIMBE TEA AUCTION DETAILS

TURNOVER - MALAWI TEA

Season	1.7.86-30.6.87	1.7.87-30.6.88	1.7.88-30.6.89	1.7.89-30.6.90
Auction	6,673,735 Kg	8,034,939 Kg	12,804,836 Kg	13,752,859 Kg
Private	1,163,535 Kg	1,908,051 Kg	2,327,604 Kg	2,752,142 Kg
Forward	-	-	-	-
Local	-	-	-	4,017 Kg
	7,837,270 Kg	9,942,990 Kg	15,132,440 Kg	14,509,081 Kg

MALAWI CROP FIGURES FOR THE SAME PERIOD

	37,819,148 Kg	33,109,245 Kg	40,779,362 Kg	42,607,678 Kg
TBCA %	20.72 %	30.03 %	37.11 %	34.05 %

Season	1.7.90-30.6.91	1.7.91-30.6.92	1.7.92-30.6.93	1.7.93-30.6.94
Auction	14,328,136 Kg	13,416,403 Kg	11,740,076 Kg	13,237,291 Kg
Private	1,478,640 Kg	734,978 Kg	1,740,631 Kg	984,746 Kg
Forward	193,320 Kg	400,600 Kg	334,500 Kg	136,700 Kg
Local	2,495 Kg	3,432 Kg	3,738 Kg	3,283 Kg
	16,002,591 Kg	14,555,413 Kg	13,818,945 Kg	14,362,020 Kg

MALAWI CROP FIGURES FOR THE SAME PERIOD

	36,991,071 Kg	36,064,975 Kg	32,117,889 Kg	39,916,391 Kg
TBCA %	43.26 %	40.36 %	43.03 %	35.98 %

Season	1.7.94-30.6.95	1.7.95-30.6.96	1.7.96-30.6.97	1.7.97-30.6.98
Auction	9,806,970 Kg	10,384,866 Kg	10,434,947 Kg	15,219,073 Kg
Private	913,514 Kg	1,006,461 Kg	1,424,677 Kg	1,759,138 Kg
Forward	224,160 Kg	228,810 Kg	100,364 Kg	15,964 Kg
Local	2,650 Kg	4,680.2Kg	4,295 Kg	7,551.5Kg
	10,947,294 Kg	11,624,817.2Kg	11,964,283 Kg	17,001,726.5Kg

MALAWI CROP FIGURES FOR THE SAME PERIOD

	34,308,674 Kg	34,751,788 Kg	38,064,261 Kg	46,102,142 Kg
TBCA %	31.91 %	33.45 %	31.43 %	36.88 %

REGIONAL TEA SALES

SEASON	ZIMBABWE	MOZAMBIQUE	ZAMBIA
1.7.86-30.6.87	Nil	Nil	Nil
1.7.87-30.6.88	297,194 Kg	Nil	Nil
1.7.88-30.6.89	487,836 Kg	13,200 Kg	Nil
1.7.89-30.6.90	71,600 Kg	142,305 Kg	Nil
1.7.90-30.6.91	Nil	Nil	13,400 Kg
1.7.91-30.6.92	24,380 Kg	Nil	89,644 Kg
1.7.92-30.6.93	Nil	Nil	Nil
1.7.93-30.6.94	Nil	Nil	Nil
1.7.94-30.6.95	55,800 kg	Nil	Nil
1.7.95-30.6.96	28,000 Kg	Nil	Nil
1.7.96-30.6.97	Nil	Nil	Nil
1.7.97-30.6.98	Nil	Nil	Nil

PROGRESS OF TEA BROKERS CENTRAL AFRICA DURING MY TWELVE YEARS AS MANAGING DIRECTOR

LIMBE AUCTION CATALOGUE PERCENTAGES

SEASON	TBCA	TCB	T&CB	TOTAL
1.7.86-30.6.87	63.31	36.69		100.00
1.7.87-30.6.88	66.26	33.74		100.00
1.7.88-30.6.89	68.47	31.53		100.00
1.7.89-30.6.90	69.31	30.69		100.00
1.7.90-30.6.91	68.86	31.14		100.00
1.7.91-30.6.92	70.40	29.60		100.00
1.7.92-30.6.93	75.45	24.55		100.00
1.7.93-30.6.94	73.96	26.04		100.00
1.7.94-30.6.95	79.78	20.22		100.00
1.7.95-30.6.96	76.81	23.19		100.00
1.7.96-30.6.97	69.51	7.84	22.65	100.00
1.7.97-30.6.98	72.68	-	27.32	100.00

TURNOVER - MALAWI COFFEE - KILOS

SEASON	AUCTION	PRIVATE	LOCAL	TOTAL
1.7.86-30.6.87	621,240 Kgs	139,860 Kgs	-	761,100 Kgs
.7.87-30.6.88	516,558 Kgs	212,265 Kgs	-	728,823 Kgs
1.7.88-30.6.89	579,360 Kgs	166,459 Kgs	-	745,819 Kgs
1.7.89-30.6.90	196,851 Kgs	61 Kgs	140	197,052 Kgs
1.7.90-30.6.91	81,241 Kgs	87,900 Kgs	88	169,229 Kgs
1.7.91-30.6.92	36,000 Kgs	102,000 Kgs	58	138,058 Kgs
1.7.92-30.6.93	-	6,660 Kgs	-	6,660 Kgs
1.7.93-30.6.94	-	-	-	Nil
1.7.94-30.6.95	-	-	-	Nil
1.7.95-30.6.96	-	-	-	Nil
1.7.96-30.6.97	-	12,533 Kgs	-	12,533 Kgs
1.7.97-30.6.98	-	45,427 Kgs	-	45,427 Kgs

COMMODITIES - KILOS

SEASON	CHILLIES	TURMERIC	CITRONELLA	SESAME(S)	ANATO	CARDOMOM	SUNFLOWER	PEPPER
1986/87	-	-	-	-	-	-	-	-
1987/88	-	-	-	-	-	-	-	-
'88/89	47,345	1,310	-	-	-	-	-	-
1989/90	-	-	-	-	-	-	-	-
1990/91	3,093.30	-	111 Lts	630	30.50	-	-	-
1991/92	-	-	487 Lts	-	-	726	880	438
1992/93	-	-	278 Lts	-	-	162.50	-	-
1993/94	-	-	27 Lts	-	-	160.15	-	20
1994/95	-	-	-	-	-	-	-	-
1995/96	-	-	-	-	-	60	-	140
1996/97	-	-	-	-	-	-	-	-
1997/98	150	-	-	-	-	-	-	-

Additionally, 151 kilos of Katambora Rhodes Grass Seed was sold in 1991/92.

TEA BROKERS CENTRAL AFRICA LTD.

P.O. BOX 5543, LIMBE, MALAWI

Telephone BLANTYRE: 640 344

Telex: 44149 TEABROCA MI
Fax: 640 462

Directors:

T.D. Clifton (Chairman)
P. Guston (Managing Director)
P.M. Chagwa
R. Wrixen
S.B. Zidana

ADDENDUM TO REPORT

In Association With
Wilson, Smithett & Co. London
Africa Tea Brokers Ltd. Nairobi

TEA YEAR 1ST JULY 1997 – 30TH JUNE 1998

RECORD TOTALS ACHIEVED		PREVIOUS HIGHEST FIGURE AND SEASON	
1) PROFIT BEFORE TAX K6.827 Million		K 1,058,907	1.7.94 – 30.6.95
2) TURNOVER			
17,001,726 Kilos		16,002,591 Kgs	1.7.90 – 30.6.91

3) RECORD WEEK 12TH – 17TH JANUARY, 1998

BROKERAGE

AUCTION USD	27,065.52 @ 21.5686	Kwacha	583,765.37
PRIVATE USD	3,484.06	Kwacha	75,146.30
USD	30,549.58	Kwacha	658,911.67

TURNOVER

AUCTION USD 1,353,276.00	Kwacha	29,188,268.73
PRIVATE USD 174,203.00	Kwacha	3,757,314.83
USD 1,527,479.00	Kwacha	32,945,583.56

KILOS SOLD:

AUCTION	861,140.00	Kgs
PRIVATE	160,400.00	Kgs
TOTAL	1,021,540	Kgs

4) LARGEST CATALOGUE			
AUCTION NO. 35	28.4.98	AUCTION NO. 21	14.1.92
	18,220 Packages		18,140 Packages

5) SAMPLE TEA RETURNS			
	7,551.50 Kilos	4,680.2 Kilos	1.7.95 – 30.6.96

YEAR	GROSS	TAX	NETT PROFIT	DIVIDEND PER SHARE
1.7.84 – 30.6.85	K 229,115	110,151	118,964	K0.75
1.7.85 – 30.6.86	-	-	(36,450)	-
1.7.86 – 30.6.87	Extraordinary Item	7,274	24,114	K0.10
1.7.87 – 30.6.88	K 43,662	32,695	10,967	K0.10
1.7.88 – 30.6.89	K 206,679	95,111	111,568	K1.00
1.7.89 – 30.6.90	K 260,660	119,427	141,233	K1.50
1.7.90 – 30.6.91	K 134,538	60,432	74,106	K0.50
1.7.91 – 30.6.92	K 105,952	52,168	53,784	K0.50
1.7.92 – 30.6.93	K 500,366	194,738	305,628	K2.00
1.7.93 – 30.6.94	K 504,225	172,944	331,281	K3.00
1.7.94 – 30.6.95	K 1,058,907	412,136	646,771	K7.00
1.7.95 – 30.6.96	K 538,043	294,955	243,088	K5.00
1.7.96 – 30.6.97	K 1,051,498	405,903	475,416	K6.00
1.7.97 – 30.6.98	K 6,826,727	2,597,928	4,228,799	K53.37

ROBBIE

A FAITHFUL COMPANION

APPENDIX
HOMEWARD BOUND

L'Agulhas

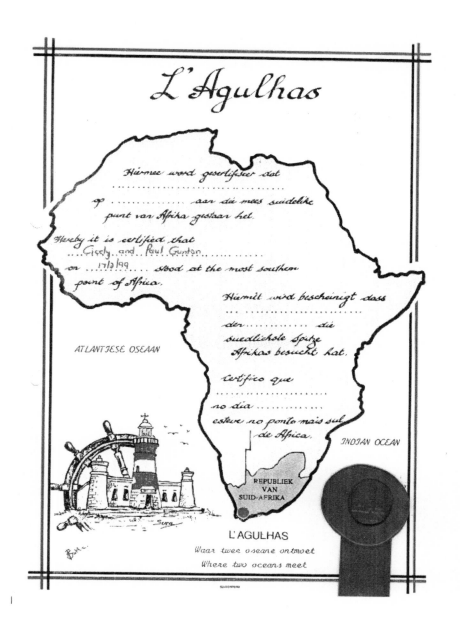

Hiermee word gesertifiseer dat
....
op .... aan die mees suidelike
punt van Afrika gestaar het.

Hereby it is certified that
.....Cicely and Paul Gunton..................
on ....17/2/99.... stood at the most southern
point of Africa.

Hiermit wird bescheinigt dass
... ...
der............ die
suedlichste Spitze
Afrikas besucht hat.

Certifico que
....
no dia ....
esteve no ponto mais sul
de Africa.

ATLANTIESE OSEAAN

INDIAN OCEAN

REPUBLIEK
VAN
SUID-AFRIKA

L'AGULHAS
Waar twee oseane ontmoet
Where two oceans meet

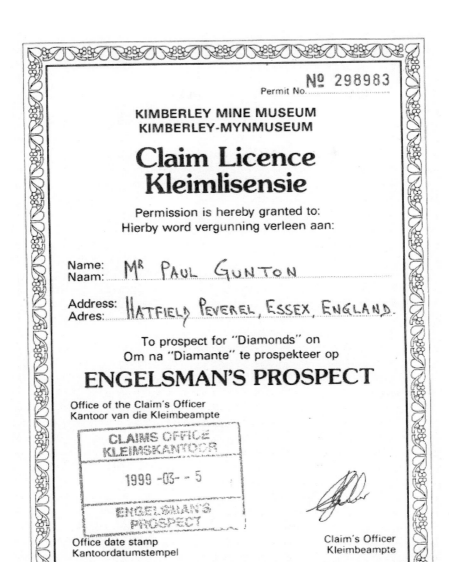

Permit No. **№ 298983**

KIMBERLEY MINE MUSEUM
KIMBERLEY-MYNMUSEUM

Claim Licence
Kleimlisensie

Permission is hereby granted to:
Hierby word vergunning verleen aan:

Name: MR PAUL GUNTON
Naam:

Address: HATFIELD PEVEREL, ESSEX, ENGLAND.
Adres:

To prospect for "Diamonds" on
Om na "Diamante" te prospekteer op

ENGELSMAN'S PROSPECT

Office of the Claim's Officer
Kantoor van die Kleimbeampte

CLAIMS OFFICE
KLEIMSKANTOOR

1999 -03- - 5

ENGELSMAN'S
PROSPECT

Office date stamp
Kantoordatumstempel

Claim's Officer
Kleimbeampte

SwiftPrint 9708

205

ABOUT THE AUTHOR

Paul Gunton was born on the 27th October 1938 in Bromsgrove and educated at Abberley Hall and Blundells School, settling off on his adventures aged twenty years old. Married with two sons and three grandchildren he now lives in the west of Ireland with his wife Cicely, continues to shave every morning with the Eclipse razor his father gave to him when he was fifteen years old and is quite content without the use of a watch, mobile telephone, computer and all associated equipment – as confirmed in his letter published in the Global Weekly Telegraph newspaper issue No 866, period 27th February – 4th March 2008:-

Passwords? No way

SIR – I have absolute sympathy for the three correspondents (letters, Issue 860) who complained about the number of passwords they have to remember.

However, these gentlemen may take a leaf out of my book for I have retired to the West of Ireland and have no need of a watch, mobile phone, let alone a computer. I am blessed with not having to remember a string of passwords and, with 3,000 miles of Atlantic ocean nearby, the air is fresh, the traffic sparse.

P Gunton
Ballymote, Co Sligo, Ireland.

Lightning Source UK Ltd.
Milton Keynes UK
24 November 2009

146656UK00001B/210/P